GOD

IS NOT

YOUR

PROBLEM

GOD

IS NOT

YOUR

PROBLEM

BILLY JOE DAUGHERTY

DESTINY IMAGE® PUBLISHERS, INC.
P.O. Box 310, Shippensburg, PA 17257-0310

"Speaking to the Purposes of God for This Generation and for the Generations to Come"

This book and all other Destiny Image, Revival Press, MercyPlace, Fresh Bread, Destiny Image Fiction, and Treasure House books are available at Christian bookstores and distributors worldwide.

For a U.S. bookstore nearest you, call 1-800-722-6774.
For more information on foreign distributors, call 717-532-3040.

Or reach us on the Internet:
www.destinyimage.com

ISBN 10: 0-7684-2347-3
ISBN 13: 978-0-7684-2347-1
Previously published as ISBN 1-56267-464-1

For Worldwide Distribution, Printed in the U.S.A.

1 2 3 4 5 6 7 8 9 10 11 / 09 08 07 06

CONTENTS

INTRODUCTION

Some people think that God is their problem. Whether deliberately, very negatively, or even subconsciously, many people have felt at times that God was allowing, permitting, or giving access for evil to come into their lives.

This type of thinking will bring alienation from God. It will also cause your faith to become dull. How can you approach God if you think He is your problem? How can you have a love relationship with Him if you think He is an adversary to you?

The way you think affects the way you believe, and the way you think and believe affects the way you speak. When you think, believe, and speak something, you will begin to act it out. We live in the experience of our thinking, our believing, and our speaking. So in order for us to change our life experiences and what is happening to us, we have to change our thinking.

Right now there are millions of people who are disconnected from the church and from God because in one way or another, there has been an implication that God is the One who has caused their problems. Therefore, they don't want anything to do with Him.

Where there have been premature deaths of family members, calamities, tragedies, sickness, disease, poverty, broken homes, and marriages, some people may not directly blame God, yet they say, "Well, God allowed it." It's as if they believe God sanctioned it.

Many people tolerate church attendance because in their hearts and minds they know that's where they need to be. They read their Bibles, yet in their hearts, there is an alienation from the loving kindness of God because of a misrepresentation of His character.

This book exposes wrong thinking, believing, and speaking. You will receive help to correct these areas and align them with the truth of God's Word, which is His will, and magnify His goodness. I want to help remove the misinformation so you are free, and I also want to equip you so you will be able to set other people free.

Among the topics this book will cover in order to get God's character and nature straight in our hearts and minds are: Paul's thorn in the flesh; Job's challenges; the sovereignty of God; the free will of man; ruling your own spirit; satan has already been defeated; being a part of God's family; the results of obedience as well as disobedience to the Word of God; and walking in the authority that Jesus Christ has invested in you through His death, burial, and resurrection.

It is time to rise up in every area of your life! Because of what you have experienced, you may think you are down for the count. But, as a born-again believer, the good news is that the same power that raised Christ from the dead dwells in you! This means that nothing can keep you down! It means that nothing God has ordained for you will be withheld from you if you are walking in obedience to the principles of His Word.

One of the key principles presented is that you must be in submission to authority figures in your life—Christ first and foremost—for you to be placed in a position of authority. You must know of your inheritance in Christ and your position in Him. Then, you must be submitted to the Word of God and to the Spirit of God, as well as to the authority figures in government, business, church, and family.

God wants you to live in dominion and authority in your personal life as well as in your public life, giving the devil no place in any area of your life. The triumph that Jesus achieved in His death, burial, and resurrection is your triumph! It is up to you to enforce satan's defeat and Christ's victory!

In this book, *God Is Not Your Problem*, the issue will be settled that God and the devil are not working together to refine your character. They are not working together in a coalition team. They are opponents! You will also settle the issue that God is a loving Father who has a beautiful plan for your life. He wants you to have His very best! Once you understand these truths, it will be much easier to surrender your will and agenda to God's will and plan for your life.

As you rise up in the fullness of the authority God has invested in you, you will realize that *God is not your problem!* He is your Answer regarding every situation you will ever be confronted with in life. He and His promises are unchanging, never subject to change.

As you trust in Jesus Christ, get rid of all doubt and unbelief, and apply the principles in this book, you will begin to soar like an eagle to higher heights in Him!

CHAPTER 1

JESUS AND SATAN ARE OPPONENTS

In John 10:10, Jesus very clearly identifies the origin of good and evil: "The thief [the devil or satan] does not come except to steal, and to kill, and to destroy. I [Jesus] have come that they may have life, and that they may have it more abundantly." *Abundant life is the will of God for you!* In John 10, verse 11, Jesus said, "I am the good shepherd. The good shepherd gives His life for the sheep."

These verses give a very clear picture of God on one side bringing goodness and abundance, and the devil on the other side stealing, killing, and destroying. It is important for you to understand that Jesus and the devil are not working together. There is no secret coalition between them.

Abundant life is the will of God for you!

The devil was an archangel of God. He rebelled against God because of pride (see Ezek. 28 and Isa. 14). He led a third of the angels in that rebellion. Satan is identified in Scripture as the destroyer, liar, thief, and murderer. He rebelled against God and he has never changed. Jesus and the devil are not partners.

Here is the issue. The Lord is not using the devil to do His work—to develop you, to train you, or to prepare you. Jesus is not using the enemy to discipline you or to correct you. That is a fairly ridiculous thought when you actually think about it. What loving father or mother would let a perverted criminal, thief, or murderer discipline their children? No matter how bad the child has been, you would never turn him or her into the hands of someone like that.

Now, if we have this much understanding of an earthly father, how much more will our heavenly Father guard, deliver, and protect us?

We acknowledge that there are bad things that have happened to people. I am not saying that the devil has not affected, touched, influenced, or impacted people. He has, but what is important is that *we do not blame God!*

When Adam and Eve sinned, a corruption came into the earth that affected all of creation. God did not plan to put beautiful people on the earth, then kill them with hurricanes or destroy them with tornadoes or some other disaster. God's plan is good from beginning to end. God is a good God, and He has good plans for you.

GOD IS NOT THE CAUSE OF UNTIMELY DEATHS

When Charles Story, who heads our prison ministry at Victory Christian Center, was ten years old, his mother died of an illness. In the middle of the night he was awakened by a minister who said to him, "Son, God has taken your mother home to be with Him." Charles said that at that moment, he cursed that minister and cursed God, vowing he would never enter a church again.

Charles kept his word for 46 years. His wife had been listening to us on the radio, and she had started attending Victory. She talked Charles into coming. Charles was a compulsive gambler, and he was living his life in a totally different direction from God. When he came to Victory, he gave his life to Jesus Christ and then attended our Bible college.

Now in his seventies, Charles travels across Oklahoma preaching in the prisons and helping to establish Victory Bible Institutes in the prisons. Thank God for redemption!

Why do I tell you this story? Charles represents a lot of people in the way they feel about church, about God, and about Christians. For 46 years Charles had the view that for some reason God had just snatched his mother out of the earth with a horrible disease and He wrecked their family. It didn't make sense to Charles, yet that is what he was told. He wanted nothing to do with a God whom he perceived to be the killer of his mother.

There is a huge difference between God *taking* someone and God *receiving* someone. Jesus said in John 14 that He was going to prepare a place for us and that He would receive us unto Himself at the time of our home-going.

> *Let not your heart be troubled; you believe in God, believe also in Me. In My Father's house are many mansions; if it were not so, I would have told you. I go to prepare a place for you. And if I go and prepare a place for you, I will come again and* **receive** *you to Myself; that where I am, there you may be also* (John 14:1-3).

There is a time to die, but there is a course we are to finish before we leave this planet. God has a number of days for us to fulfill. There are things that can shorten life and there are things that can lengthen it. Proverbs cites many different ways of how to lengthen the days of our life and how God will do it as we act on His wisdom.

What is important for us is that *we do not perceive God as the One who is against us.* God is not our problem, and He is not against us. God is for us more than we are for us. He loves us more than we love ourselves. He wants the best for us more than we want the best for us. His love is truly amazing. It was God's amazing grace that sent His Son to die in our place, to suffer for us, and then to be raised from the dead so we could have eternal life.

It is important that we look at the whole counsel of God. We can find bad things that happened at certain times in history. We need to ask ourselves, "Are we living under the principles and laws of the same time frame? Do we have the same situation?"

GOOD AND PERFECT GIFTS COME FROM GOD

In James 1:12-17, James contributes to the clarity of the sources of evil and of good:

> *Blessed is the man who endures* [and overcomes] *temptation; for when he has been approved, he will receive the crown of life which the Lord has promised to those who love Him. Let no one say when he is tempted, "I am tempted by God";* **for God cannot be tempted by evil, nor does He Himself tempt anyone.** [If temptation is coming at you, don't identify it as coming from God.] *But each one is tempted when he is drawn away by his own desires and enticed. Then, when desire has conceived, it brings forth sin; and sin, when it is full-grown, brings forth death. Do not be deceived, my beloved brethren. Every good gift and every perfect gift is from above, and comes down from the Father of lights, with whom there is no variation or shadow of turning.*

God is good all the time, and the devil is bad all the time.

Don't get them mixed up!

James makes it very clear: Every good gift and every perfect gift come from the Father. God is good all the time, and the devil is bad all the time. Don't get them mixed up!

SOURCES OF BAD PROBLEMS

There are three primary sources of where bad things come from. You need to be able to identify them.

1. Satan, or the demonic realm, demon spirits, the whole realm of darkness.

2. Sometimes what other people do affects us (i.e., their lack of knowledge, sin, failures, and/or mistakes).

3. Our own lack of knowledge, sin, failures, and/or mistakes.

The earth is not in the place of beauty and total synchronization that it was in when it was first created. Man's sin and the rebellion of satan affected planet Earth. We still see the beauty and the glory that God created, but there is far more that we don't see. We will see the original when we see Heaven, because the earth was patterned after it. One day we'll see the earth in the way that God intended and planned, far beyond what it is today.

Think about it! God planned the raindrops with you in mind. He formed the ocean with you in mind. He designed the mountains and the rivers with you on His mind. God wanted the lights at night to be so spectacular for you that He spoke them into existence by the billions and put each star in place! He set planet Earth the right distance from the sun so we wouldn't be scorched and we wouldn't freeze. When we begin to think about creation, we begin to realize: we have a Father who has our very best interests at heart.

Think about your ears that He created. He put them in just the right place. What if He had turned them upward? Then, when it rained, you wouldn't be able to hear! Your pancreas, your liver, and your immune system are in place by design. Think of all the intricacies of how you were "fearfully

> *We have a Father who has our very best interests at heart.*

and wonderfully made" (Ps. 139:14). God was thinking of you every moment of creation, and He hasn't stopped thinking about you! Glory to God!

MALIGNING GOD'S CHARACTER

When we look at situations that face us and others today, whether it be temptations, tests, trials, disasters, calamities, and/or tragedies, the important thing for us to remember is that *we shouldn't blame God.*

Think about it. If someone starts talking about your mama or your daddy, saying bad things about them, how do you feel? Yet, some of God's children have talked about Him and said that He did this and He did that. They have given a bad image of Him to others. One word that is used to describe what these people have done it is "slander"—maligning God's character.

Time and time again I have talked to people who say, "If God is such a great God as you say, why all these wars? Why are so many people sick? Why is there all this trouble in the earth?" In other words, in their mind, God is the one who is causing all of these problems. They go on and say some bad things or share about a tragedy that happened to a family member.

The first thing you need to say is, "God didn't do it." Their alienation from God comes from their perception that God is their problem, that God is the one who caused all of the difficulties.

In John 10:10, Jesus promised "abundant life" while satan is identified as the sinister force of evil who has affected the whole of creation, other people, and even our own lives.

Jesus said in the Lord's Prayer that we should pray that God's will in Heaven be done here in the earth. Think about it. How much evil is going on in Heaven? None! So how much evil does God want in our lives here in the earth? None! He made it very clear, "I want Heaven's will done right here on the earth." So how good is Heaven? It's very good! How good does God want it for you and me in the earth? Very good!

When you believe that, you will position yourself to receive the goodness of God and refuse what is not from God. Many times people have closed themselves to God's goodness and opened themselves to the devil's badness because of wrong thinking. As a result of having been lied to and hearing bad things about God, they have turned away from God. They have embraced darkness, calamity, and tragedy, and all types of things have literally followed their lives. They thought these things were from God and they blamed Him.

When Jesus came teaching, preaching, healing, and delivering, the religious leaders began to say, "By the ruler of the demons He casts out demons" (Mark 3:22). Jesus' response was, "How can Satan cast out Satan? If a kingdom is divided against itself, that kingdom cannot stand" (Mark 3:23-24).

Just because something happens to you doesn't mean it's the will of God.

Jesus and the devil are not on the same team. There are people who have identified the gifts of the Spirit, miracles, healing, and speaking in other tongues as being of the devil. However, the truth is, those are gifts of the Holy Spirit to help the Body of Christ (see 1 Cor. 12).

At other times, the works of the devil—accidents, calamities, and tragedies—have been attributed to God. People have the devil and God mixed up. In this process, they have rejected what God wanted to do to help them and accepted what satan was sending against them.

It is very important in this hour that we get it settled. If you think that evil, attacks, or sickness have come from God or that God said to the devil, "It's okay for you to attack My children them," then *how can you resist those attacks?*

If you think that a work of evil or an attack has been sent from God to develop your character, to train you, to prepare you, to purify you, and to shape your personality, and you think that God either is doing it or He has given the devil permission to do it, then how can you pray for it to be removed? People who believe this way have no resistance against the attacks, because they say, "This must be the will of God." Just because something happens to you doesn't mean it's the will of God.

Just suppose something is sent from the enemy to teach you, and it's disaster, calamity, or tragedy; how do you know when you have learned enough? Just think about it! That's the dilemma many people find themselves in.

I have talked with people who have this misunderstanding of God. I ask them, "How do you know when you are going to be able to be over it?" "Well, I don't know" is the usual reply. When our thinking gets distorted and we don't know where an attack is from or why it has come and we assume that God is behind it, we find ourselves in a position from which it is very difficult to pray for healing, deliverance, protection, and preservation, or to resist the attack in any way.

It is important for us to know that God teaches us with His Word, He instructs us by His Spirit, and the Spirit will guide us into all truth. God uses godly people to teach His principles, not demonic spirits, calamities, tragedies, disasters, or things that would come against us. Those things are sent to destroy.

So what about Job's life? Simply stated, he was blessed by God, he was attacked by satan, and then God blessed him again. We will examine his life in the next chapter to gain further clarity of the goodness of God and the badness of the devil.

CHAPTER 2

———— WHAT ABOUT JOB? ————

One of the classic questions that people ask is, "What about Job? Didn't the devil ask permission to attack Job and God gave him permission?" We need to understand three things about Job's story:

1. God blessed Job;

2. The devil attacked Job; and

3. After Job prayed for his friends, God blessed Job with twice as much as he had before.

God blessed Job in the beginning and at the end. Satan attacked Job in the middle of his life. If you get these facts straight, that will help you with the Book of Job.

One of the things we need to understand about Job's situation is that Job lived during a time when they did not have the Bible. We also know that Job lived during a time when they did not have the New Covenant that we have today. Jesus had not come yet. This is why Job said, "Nor is there any mediator between us..." (Job 9:33). There was no one between Job and God to make that connection and to help him have understanding. The Holy Spirit could not dwell inside of him because the Holy Spirit had not been sent yet to indwell every believer.

In Job 3:25, Job he said, "For the thing I greatly feared has come upon me...." Fear attracts just like faith attracts. Job was an upright, holy, godly man, but because of an occurrence that happened with his children that is described in Job, chapter 1, he declared that what he had feared had come upon him.

Long after Job lived, Jesus came and paid for our sins on the cross, was buried, and raised from the dead. In His death, burial, and resurrection, He disarmed all of the principalities and powers of darkness. He took the keys of dominion back that Adam and Eve had lost. Jesus restored it back for everyone who would believe in Him.

We need to honor Job for his integrity, steadfastness, and patience, but we are living in a totally different time period, and we have a much better covenant than Job (see Heb. 8:6).

THE POWER OF THE NEW COVENANT

Let's look at the power of the New Covenant so when you face situations, you will realize, "I am not in the same position as Job. Yes, I want to follow his steadfastness, patience, endurance, and integrity. But thank God, just as Job said, 'I know that my Redeemer lives...' (Job 19:25), I can say, 'I know my Redeemer lives and He has paid for my sins and delivered me from satan's kingdom.'"

Job could not say that, not because he didn't want to, but it had not happened yet. It had nothing to do with his character, abilities, integrity, or righteousness. Those were all intact, but it was the time period. So when you identify with Job, make sure you do it from a clear biblical standpoint with the whole counsel of God.

Colossians 1:12 says, "Giving thanks to the Father who has qualified us to be partakers of the inheritance of the saints in the light." When Jesus died, He qualified us to get in on His inheritance. What is our inheritance? God gave us everything that is in Him. We have His nature, His life, His love, His peace, and His joy. We are now heirs of God and joint heirs with Jesus Christ. This inheritance was not available until Jesus died, so Job had no access to it.

Colossians 1:13 states, "He has delivered us from the power of darkness...." When Jesus paid for our sins on the cross, He literally brought us out from satan's kingdom "...and conveyed us into the kingdom of the Son of His love" (Col. 1:13). Job did not have this provision. Verse 14 says, "In whom we have redemption through His blood, the forgiveness of sins."

Was it possible for Job to have his sins blotted out totally? No. The best he had was animal sacrifices where sins were covered. We have a New Covenant in which our sins are blotted out. We are redeemed. We were purchased out from satan's authority and delivered into the Kingdom of light. We are under a whole new rule and reign of authority.

Does the New Testament say that we should embrace evil or lay hold of tragedies, calamities, and disasters? No! Paul said, "Put on the whole armor of God, that you may be able to stand against the wiles of the devil" (Eph. 6:11).

Paul also said, "Above all, taking the shield of faith with which you will be able to quench all the fiery darts of the wicked one" (Eph. 6:16). James said, "Submit to God. Resist the devil and he will flee from you" (James 4:7). Peter said, "Be sober, be vigilant; because your adversary the devil walks about like a roaring lion, seeking whom he may devour. Resist him, steadfast in the faith..." (1 Pet. 5:8-9).

Then, in John's first Epistle, he said, "We know that whoever is born of God does not sin; but he who has been born of God keeps himself, and the wicked one does not touch him" (1 John 5:18).

This is New Testament thinking. It is not God's will for you to be delivered over into the hands of the enemy for a few days or a few weeks to teach you, train you, test you, or beat up on you to see what's inside of you! We need to learn from Job's patience and his endurance, but understand that we have a New Covenant that he did not possess.

In the Lord's Prayer, Jesus said to pray, "Do not lead us into temptation, but deliver us from the evil one…" (Matt. 6:13). It is God's will that we be delivered from evil and rescued out of the hand of the enemy. We can stop the works of darkness with our faith and have the assurance that we are not going to get friendly fire from our Father! ("Friendly fire" is a term used in the military for when you are fighting and your own people start shooting at you.) This is why a lot of people have bailed out of church. They have been told, "That's God shooting at you!"

Evil attacks that steal, kill, or destroy do not come from God. They may have come from our own mistakes, the mistakes of others, the fallen nature of the earth, or they could have come from the enemy, but *don't identify God as your problem*. He loves you, He cares for you, and He wants the best for you.

It is time that we as believers stand up together, lock our shields, and say, "We are stopping the fiery darts of the wicked. Every person in our family is going to finish their days. No one else is going home early."

It is our hour to rise up and believe for one another. Other people need your faith and your prayers. You don't need to be throttled and shut down and say, "I don't know what's going to happen." You need your faith turned up strong to believe in a good God and to stand on the promises of His Word and not waver on either His *willingness* or His *ability* to perform His Word.

CHAPTER 3

ROADBLOCKS TO SURRENDERING TO THE LORD

To fully experience God's goodness, you must fully surrender to the Lord. Are you fully surrendered to the Lord? Is there an area of your life that you haven't fully surrendered to Him? Jesus surrendered His will to the Father in the Garden of Gethsemane: "Not My will, but Yours, be done" (Luke 22:42).

In Paul's writings to the Philippian church, he said:

Let this mind be in you which was also in Christ Jesus,

Who, being in the form of God, did not consider it robbery to be equal with God,

But made Himself of no reputation, taking the form of a bond servant, and coming in the likeness of men.

And being found in appearance as a man, He humbled Himself and became obedient to the point of death, even the death of the cross.

Therefore God also has highly exalted Him and given Him the name which is above every name,

That at the name of Jesus every knee should bow, of those in heaven, and of those on earth, and of those under the earth,

And that every tongue should confess that Jesus Christ is Lord, to the glory of God the Father (Philippians 2:5-11).

Jesus humbled Himself to obey His Father. That is what *surrender* means. Surrendering takes humility, a brokenness, a yieldedness, a willingness to do the Father's will.

IDENTIFYING ROADBLOCKS

Each person has a choice as to whether or not he or she will surrender to the will of the Lord. There are a lot of reasons why people don't surrender. Probably at the top of the list is *pride*. That's what brought lucifer down.

Out of pride comes *rebellion* and rebellion's twin, *stubbornness*. When people are proud, rebellious, and stubborn, they are demonstrating that their fear of what other people think is greater than their fear of God.

Thus, *Fear* is another cause that you can add to your list of reasons as to why people do not surrender to the Lord.

Another reason is *selfishness*. People want their own way. They want to do their own thing. They want to run their own life. Why would they want someone else to lord over them or rule over their life? So they do not surrender.

There are a few other reasons why people don't surrender to the Lord. One of them is *all the hypocrites!* A lot of people would surrender, but they know some person who said they were a Christian or who goes to church who did something wrong or didn't do something they should have. So people use, "There are so many hypocrites," as an excuse for not surrendering.

It is rather amusing to listen to someone talk about the "other" hypocrites. It is humorous to me to hear them say, "There are so many hypocrites." Usually the way this person covers himself or herself for not surrendering to the Lord is by saying, "At least I am real." My question has always been, "Real what?" What is the difference between a real sinner and a real hypocrite? Both have missed the boat!

Why would you let another person keep you from God? What does their failure or lack of doing something have to do with you? Some people have a 30-year list of hypocrites on a computer printout. It is amazing to me how people can find the speck in other people's eyes, yet fail to see the telephone pole in their own eyes! That is a hindrance or a roadblock that will keep many people from surrendering to God.

Another reason for not surrendering to the Lord is *procrastination*. "I'll do it tomorrow." "I'm thinking about it." "I'll consider it." "I'm not ready yet." "One of these days." "When I get around to it." Always putting something in tomorrow excuses you from a decision today. That's why a lot of people don't surrender.

Another reason people use, and the one I want to focus on, has affected millions of people, and that is, **blaming God for problems in their life**. Many people think that God is behind calamities, tragedies, and disasters that have hit either them or a loved one. Therefore people resist surrendering because, after all, why would they surrender to someone who has harmed them or harmed one of their loved ones?

Many times people don't say this verbally, but subconsciously it is in the back of their mind: "This happened to so-and-so." They don't know whether they want to submit and surrender to what they perceive to be from God. God has been blamed for a lot of things that were not from Him.

Many people, especially in insurance companies, speak of natural disasters as being "acts of God," as if God sent the tornado, hurricane, or storm to destroy a town or a home. This perception has kept many from complete surrender to God.

BREAKING FREE OF ROADBLOCKS

There are many things that will help us get free of these road-blocks. Here are a few important ones to remember.

When God made the earth, He made it perfect and beautiful. But when satan rebelled and then led Adam and Eve in rebellion against God, even the earth itself was affected, and corruption came as a result.

What we are experiencing now is not the fullness of what God originally planned. We still see the beauty of the earth—the oceans, the mountains, the rivers, the trees, the grass, the birds, the fish, and all that is here—yet, originally earth was made as a replica of Heaven. One day we will see it as it was intended to be. The Bible says that all of the earth groans under this burden of what happened as a result of the fall. The earth is waiting for the manifestation of the sons of God.

When God created man, He gave him dominion. When Adam sinned, he transferred that dominion into satan's hands. That is where wars, calamities, tragedies, disease, and disaster come from. Not by the will and purpose of God, but because God gave man free will, and then man made wrong choices.

God is not your problem. He is the Problem Solver!

It is very important that *you do not blame God for the challenges you are facing.* God is not your problem. He is the Problem Solver! He is not the one who hurt you. He is the One who heals, helps, and lifts. He is not the one who demonizes people. He is the One who delivers people from demons. He is not behind your troubles. He is the answer for every situation you are facing.

We must hear about Jesus, believe in Him, and then receive, submit, and surrender to Him to experience His lordship in our lives. Although Jesus regained the authority from satan, He does not force His will upon people.

He stands at the door of our heart and knocks, as Revelation 3:20 states: "Behold, I stand at the door and knock. If anyone hears My voice and opens the door, I will come in to him and dine with him, and he with Me." When we let Him in, He will begin to rule and we can walk free of satan's dominion and authority here in the earth.

This is why Jesus said, "If you abide in My word, you are My disciples indeed. And you shall know the truth, and the truth shall make you free" (John 8:31-32). It is important that we know what the Word of God says and that we let the Word set us free from all of satan's authority.

Satan Is the Oppressor

While Peter was preaching in the house of Cornelius, in the middle of his message, we find this powerful truth: "How God anointed Jesus of Nazareth with the Holy Spirit and with power, who went about doing good and healing all who were oppressed by the devil, for God was with Him" (Acts 10:38).

The devil is identified as the oppressor. He oppresses with sickness and disease. The One who does good is God, who anointed His Son Jesus with the Holy Spirit. We see the Trinity in this verse: God the Father anointed His Son with the Holy Spirit to go and do good. Doing good is healing. Sickness and disease are an oppression, so Jesus went about doing good and "healing all who were oppressed by the devil...."

Don't get God and the devil mixed up! Some people have thought that God makes people sick to train them, teach them, develop them, and shape their character. Other people have said that people who heal the sick are of the devil. Both of these are deceptions. God is good all the time, and the devil is bad all the time. So get it straight! God is the One doing the healing, and the enemy is the one who is oppressing with sickness and disease.

YOU HAVE AUTHORITY IN JESUS' NAME

Some people have even said that sickness may be the will of God at times, or that God allows the devil to attack people. Think about it. If a schoolteacher gave permission to a perverted criminal to come into her students' lives to teach them character, what kind of a teacher would she be? Deranged!

Yet, there are people who have made this type of accusation about God, that God would deliberately give the devil permission to do anything to His children. We need to understand, *God gave man dominion, but He also gave man a free will.* God lets man make his own choices.

The first Adam released that dominion into satan's hands. The second Adam, Jesus Christ, took it back in His death, burial, and resurrection. After He was raised from the dead, Jesus said, "All authority has been given to Me in heaven and on earth" (Matt. 28:18). If we will receive this authority in the name of Jesus, we can stand up against the works of satan in our homes and families. (We will deal more fully on the issue of walking in your authority and dominion in a later chapter.)

It is very hard to resist something if you think that God may have given it to you. In addition, it is very hard to surrender to someone you think might be against you. This is why a lot of people have failed to surrender to Jesus Christ. They think God is the one who did this bad thing, let them down, or didn't come through at a certain time. I'm telling you, God always comes through. But He comes through in our lives *where faith and love are working together!*

God does not force Himself on people. He has given man free will, and when we make the decision to believe and walk in love, God's glory will flood our lives.

The will of God on earth is the same as it is for Heaven. This is verified in the Lord's Prayer: "Your kingdom come. Your will be done on earth as it is in heaven" (Matt. 6:10). How much sickness, disease, calamity, and tragedy are in Heaven? None! How much does God want on earth? None! This will set you free, so lay hold of it!

God always comes through.

CHAPTER 4

WHAT ABOUT PAUL'S THORN IN THE FLESH?

One of the big issues often brought up is, "What about Paul's thorn in the flesh?" I have read and heard people say that they think Paul was made sick by God and that God told him to stay sick for His glory. When people bring up Paul's thorn, I say, "I am glad you brought it up. Let's let the Word answer the issue of Paul's thorn in the flesh."

The phrase "thorn in the flesh" comes out of the Old Testament. God told the children of Israel, "But if you do not drive out the inhabitants of the land from before you, then it shall be that those whom you let remain shall be irritants in your eyes and thorns in your side..." (Num. 33:55). He was talking about people who had a wrong spirit.

In his farewell address to the Israelites, Joshua referred to the nations fighting Israel as becoming "scourges on [the Israelites'] sides and thorns in [their] eyes...," [if the Israelites] "transgressed the covenant of the Lord [their] God..." (Josh. 23:13,16).

In Judges 2:3, the angel of the Lord said the enemies of Israel would be "thorns in your side...."

Have you ever said that someone (or something) is "a pain in the neck"? Did that mean they were sticking in your neck and their feet were dangling out? No, in English this is termed an "idiomatic expression," a phrase that describes something that is different from the words taken individually. If people drive by a place and they say, "That's an eyesore in the community," does that mean everyone gets sores in their eyes when they see it? No, again that is an idiomatic expression that we use to describe something. The "thorn in the flesh" in Second Corinthians 12:7 is an idiom describing "a messenger of Satan."

In the first few verses of Second Corinthians 12, when he was caught up into the third Heaven, Paul didn't know whether he was in his body or out of it. He just saw things that were amazing. Let's look at Second Corinthians 12:7-10:

> *And lest I should be exalted above measure by the abundance of the revelations, a thorn in the flesh was given to me, a messenger of Satan to buffet me, lest I be exalted above measure.*

> *Concerning this thing I pleaded with the Lord three times that it might depart from me.*

> *And He said to me, "My grace is sufficient for you, for My strength is made perfect in weakness." Therefore most gladly I will rather boast in my infirmities, that the power of Christ may rest upon me.*

> *Therefore I take pleasure in infirmities, in reproaches, in needs, in persecutions, in distresses, for Christ's sake. For when I am weak, then I am strong.*

Here are a few of the revelations Paul received from God:

- We become righteous by faith in Jesus Christ (see 2 Cor. 5:21).

- We are redeemed from the curse (see Gal. 3:13).

- Christ in us is the hope of glory (see Col. 1:27).

- Paul listed the gifts of the Spirit (see 1 Cor. 12).

- He explained the importance of tongues and the interpretation of tongues (see 1 Cor. 14).

- He described the Body of Christ (see 1 Cor. 12).

- He explained the purpose of the communion celebration (see 1 Cor. 11).

Wherever Paul preached, these revelations caused people to be saved, delivered, and empowered by the Holy Spirit. Why? When you know the truth, it will set you free. So everywhere Paul shared these revelations, people were getting the Kingdom of God in their lives. God's Kingdom was advancing, and Paul's impact was increasing. Paul was exalted wherever the impact of his teachings touched many lives.

Since when did God and the devil team up to develop your humility?

Paul said, "Lest I should be exalted above measure by the abundance of the revelations, a thorn in the flesh was given to me..." (2 Cor. 12:7). If God gave Paul these revelations to share and advance His Kingdom, why would God turn around and give him something to stop the revelations from getting out? He wouldn't!

Who gave this thorn in the flesh to Paul? Second Corinthians 12:7 identifies the thorn in the flesh as "a messenger of Satan"; so it was *satan* who gave it to Paul to buffet him.

Here is the real critical point, because many people say, "But God sent the devil to do that." Are God and the devil working together to develop our character? No! This question sounds rather ridiculous, but many people believe that.

Since when did God and the devil team up to develop your humility? First of all, the devil is in rebellion against God. Second, we need to understand that everything about God is in opposition to the nature of satan. They are not in a coalition together. *There is no cooperative effort between Heaven and hell to produce character inside of your life.*

The Greek word for "messenger of Satan" is *angelos*. An angel of satan is a demon spirit, which the devil sent against Paul because of the many revelations he was receiving. These revelations were changing the whole environment, and Paul was destroying the kingdom of darkness. The power and the influence of his ministry were being felt all across the known world.

There is no cooperative effort between Heaven and hell to produce character inside of your life.

God did not send an angel of satan to stop Paul. The devil sent an angel, a demonic spirit, to buffet Paul. The word *buffet* is like a ship at anchor where the waves are rocking it continually. It was a continual buffeting. Everywhere Paul went he was being hit. When you read the Book of Acts and even the epistles, you see that it didn't matter where Paul went. Sometimes people were mad at him before he even arrived. He would show up and people were upset. Sometimes while he was preaching, people would get stirred up.

Scripture says, "All who desire to live godly in Christ Jesus will suffer persecution" (2 Tim. 3:12).

Whenever you have the light and you are coming into a dark realm to set captives free, there is an enemy who does not want the captives to be set free, so there is opposition. If you stay in the same place all the time and you don't advance the Kingdom of God, you may not experience as much buffeting because you are no threat to the enemy.

Paul was not standing still. He was going into regions where the gospel had not been preached. Everywhere he went, he faced buffeting because these were areas that satan had held under his control. (This was all across Asia Minor, Ephesus, Greece, Corinth, and ultimately into Rome.)

Paul said, "I pleaded with the Lord three times that it might depart from me" (2 Cor. 12:8). I have heard people say, "God told him 'no.'" You will not find "no" anywhere in this passage. God had a different answer for him: "My grace is sufficient for you, for My strength is made perfect in weakness…" (2 Cor. 12:9).

"Grace" is God's power, help, ability, strength, love, light, gifts, and anointing—everything that God is. God was saying, "My grace is with you. Everywhere you go driving out the darkness and the enemy comes against you, My power will show up!"

Paul's response was, "Therefore most gladly I will rather boast in my infirmities, that the power of Christ may rest upon me" (2 Cor. 12:9).

"Weakness" Does Not Mean Sickness

Paul knew that every time he was in a weak situation, Christ would be strong. In this verse, "in weakness" means "in his humanity" or "in his inability." When he stood up against a demonic attack, Christ would be strong in and through him.

The word "infirmities" in this verse has to do with weakness. How do we know Paul was not talking about sickness? In Second Corinthians 11, other people were posing as apostles, and Paul tried to convince the Corinthians that he was a true apostle and that many of these people were actually false apostles:

Are they Hebrews? So am I. Are they Israelites? So am I. Are they the seed of Abraham? So am I.

Are they ministers of Christ?—I speak as a fool—I am more: in labors more abundant, in stripes above measure, in prisons more frequently, in deaths often.

From the Jews five times I received forty stripes minus one.

Three times I was beaten with rods; once I was stoned; three times I was shipwrecked; a night and a day I have been in the deep;

In journeys often, in perils of waters, in perils of robbers, in perils of my own countrymen, in perils of the Gentiles, in perils in the city, in perils in the wilderness, in perils in the sea, in perils among false brethren;

In weariness and toil, in sleeplessness often, in hunger and thirst, in fastings often, in cold and nakedness——

Besides the other things, what comes upon me daily: my deep concern for all the churches.

Who is weak, and I am not weak? Who is made to stumble, and I do not burn with indignation?

If I must boast, I will boast in the things which concern my infirmity.

The God and Father of our Lord Jesus Christ, who is blessed forever, knows that I am not lying.

In Damascus the governor, under Aretas the king, was guarding the city of the Damascenes with a garrison, desiring to arrest me;

But I was let down in a basket through a window in the wall, and escaped from his hands. (2 Corinthians 11:22-33).

In this passage of Scripture, does Paul talk about having bad eyes, cancer, or disease? No! But he does talk about being put in a weak situation in many of the places he went. Listen, when your feet are dangling in the Mediterranean as shark bait for a day and a night, you are in a weak place where only God can deliver you!

There are people who want to identify with Paul. They say, "Well, I'm like Paul. I've got this thorn in the flesh!" Most of the people who say this haven't even witnessed to one person, much less gone to another nation that doesn't know God and drive the devil out of it. We need to understand, this man Paul was penetrating realms of darkness continually. Everywhere he went, he encountered persecution. But God reassured Paul, "Everywhere you go, My grace will be sufficient for you. I will bring you through."

In Acts 14, Paul was stoned and dragged out of the city, and the mind-set of those who stoned him was "supposing him to be dead" (Acts 14:19). Verse 20 says, "However, when the disciples gathered around him, he rose up and went into the city. And the next day he departed with Barnabas to Derbe."

In Acts 16 Paul preached in Philippi. He cast the devil out of a young girl who had a fortune-telling spirit. When her owners found out she couldn't make money for them anymore, they threw Paul and Silas in prison. Paul and Silas were in a weak situation in a foreign town. They were falsely accused, beaten, and fastened in chains and stocks in the inner prison.

Paul and Silas started to sing at midnight, probably something about grace. Why? Because God said, "My grace is sufficient." I can imagine Paul saying, "Silas, we are going to have to call on God's grace right now because we are in a place that in ourselves we can't get out of. Let's magnify the Lord and thank Him for His grace."

But at midnight Paul and Silas were praying and singing hymns to God, and the prisoners were listening to them.

Suddenly there was a great earthquake, so that the foundations of the prison were shaken; and immediately all the doors were opened and everyone's chains were loosed (Acts 16:25-26).

That night Paul led the jailer and his household to Christ. The Philippian church was born out of an attack of the enemy. The devil thought he had won, but God's grace rose up in the situation.

MORE THAN CONQUERORS!

In Romans 8:37, Paul said, "Yet in all these things *we are more than conquerors through Him who loved us.*"

In Acts 27, Paul was being taken by ship to Rome where he was to appear before Caesar. There were 276 people on the ship—including, Paul, prisoners, and crewmen (see Acts 27:37).

Paul had warned the ship's crew before they ever set sail, "Men, I perceive that this voyage will end with disaster and much loss, not only of the cargo and ship, but also our lives" (Acts 27:10). His warning was ignored. An unimaginable storm came up. In the natural, all hope that the men and the ship would be saved was gone. Paul fasted and prayed, and God sent an angel to him. Then, Paul gave instructions in his famous speech from the deck of the ship:

...Men, you should have listened to me, and not have sailed from Crete and incurred this disaster and loss.

And now I urge you to take heart, for there will be no loss of life among you, but only of the ship.

For there stood by me this night an angel of the God to whom I belong and whom I serve,

Saying, "Do not be afraid, Paul; you must be brought before Caesar; and indeed God granted you all those who sail with you."

Therefore take heart, men, for I believe God that it will be just as it was told me (Acts 27:21-25).

The ship broke up, but everyone on the ship "escaped safely to land" (Acts 27:44)—to the island of Malta. All natural ability that Paul (and the other 275 men) could be saved was gone, but God's grace showed up!

However, the enemy didn't stop with this event. When Paul reached down to gather firewood on the island of Malta, a poisonous snake fastened on him. The islanders were thinking, *This is awful. First, the storm tried to get him and now the snake is going to get him!*

Acts 28:4-5 says:

So when the natives saw the creature hanging from his hand, they said to one another, "No doubt this man is a murderer, whom, though he has escaped the sea, yet justice does not allow to live."

But he [Paul] shook off the creature into the fire and suffered no harm.

When Paul didn't die, the people were ready to worship him! After Paul got the chieftain of the island healed, everyone on the island was saved. Why? God had said, "My grace is sufficient for you, for My strength is made perfect in weakness" (2 Cor. 12:9).

Paul could not be killed until his destiny was complete. In Second Timothy 4:6-7, Paul said, "The time of my departure is at hand. I have fought a good fight, I have finished the race, I have kept the faith." No one could take Paul's life. He laid it down. And I am encouraging you, don't let the devil take you out before you have finished your course!

Testimony of Jonathan Coussens

A cancerous growth was discovered on the top of Jonathan Coussens' knee. His mom, an oncology nurse, knew the seriousness of the diagnosis, but Jonathan's parents also knew what the absolute will of God was for Jonathan. They didn't question whether the tumor was from God to develop Jonathan's character, because they knew that sickness and disease do *not* come from God.

Here is Jonathan's testimony in his own words:

> Five years ago I was playing in a champions' basketball league here

Don't let the devil take you out before you have finished your course!

in Tulsa. My knee started hurting really badly. My mom, being a nurse, was like, "Oh, just ice it, take some and Ibuprofen, and it will be okay." The pain continued for another week and a half, and lying on the floor and crying, I said to my mom, "We need to go to the doctor." She was like, "All right, we'll go."

In the X-rays of my knee, the place where my growth plate should be was covered by a huge shadowy-looking thing. The doctor wrote on a piece of paper, "Go to MRI. Look for a cancerous tumor."

Mom knew exactly what he was saying with his big fancy words! We had a two-week span between the X-ray and the MRI. My mom and dad prayed with me and as an act of faith they called me "Jonathan New Knees"!

After the MRI, we went back to the doctor. As he held up the X-rays and the MRI, it was as if the blood just drained out of his face! He was like, "I can't believe it!" He pointed to the X-rays and said, "Here is the mass," and pointing to the MRI results, he said, "Here it is not!" He was totally stunned and shocked. He said, "You know, if we would have had the same thing on the MRI, we would have had to ship you off to Washington to get your leg amputated."

The Bible says that the enemy comes to steal, kill, and destroy, but God comes to give us life and life more abundantly. Romans 8:28 says, "All things work together for good to those who love God, to those who are called according to His purpose." No matter what situation you are facing, God will always bring you back on top!

During the past few months, I have been running track. Not only did God heal my knee, He made my legs fast! It has been miracle after miracle after miracle.

In his high school senior year, Jonathan finished fourth in the state in the 100-meter race. It is time to magnify the Lord for His grace and mercy.

Lord, remove every suspicion about Your goodness
and every question about Your character.
We know You are good
and You want the best for us.
I pray for every roadblock to surrender
to be removed in Jesus' name.

Give God your past, your present, and your future. Give Him your relationships and every area of your life in Jesus' name.

CHAPTER 5

THE SOVEREIGNTY OF GOD

Many people think that the bad things that have happened to them, to their family members, or in the lives of relatives and friends—the calamities, tragedies, accidents, and early deaths—have come from God. Or, they think that God gave permission to the devil to do these things.

Let's set the record straight. God is a good God all the time. Jesus said He is the Good Shepherd. The Good Shepherd doesn't kill or beat the sheep; He gives His life for the sheep. God is on the one side doing good, and the devil is on the other side doing bad.

Let's read Luke 9:51-56 as a foundation for understanding the sovereignty of God:

Now it came to pass, when the time had come for Him [Jesus] to be received up, that He steadfastly set His face to go to Jerusalem,

And sent messengers before His face. And as they went, they entered a village of the Samaritans, to prepare for Him.

But they did not receive Him, because His face was set for the journey to Jerusalem. [The Samaritans didn't like the Jews, and Jerusalem was their capital, so they didn't want Jesus coming through their village. They didn't want to meet with Him or talk to Him.]

And when His disciples James and John [who were called "the sons of thunder"] *saw this, they said, "Lord, do You want us to command fire to come down from heaven and consume them, just as Elijah did?"*

But He turned and rebuked them, and said, "You do not know what manner of spirit you are of.

"For the Son of Man did not come to destroy men's lives but to save them."

James and John had traveled with Jesus and they had experienced His miracles. They had even operated in the power of God as He sent them out to do the work of the ministry. In their evaluation, this bunch (the Samaritans) should be roasted and toasted! But Jesus said, "You do not know what manner of spirit you are of" (Luke 9:55). They weren't operating in the Spirit of God, for Jesus said He "did not come to destroy men's lives but to save them" (Luke 9:56).

James' and John's viewpoint reflects the view of many people today, and that is, if you mess up, God is going to get you. If you have done wrong, God is coming with some type of calamity or tragedy. Other people look back on bad things that have happened to other people or in their own family and they say, "God did that because of...." They have a list of reasons. As Jesus said, you do not know what manner of spirit you are of to think this way.

Think of the most famous passage of Scripture in the entire Bible, John 3:16: "For God so loved the world that He gave His only begotten Son, that whoever believes in Him should not perish but have everlasting life." Verse 17 says, "For God did not send His Son into the world to condemn the world, but that the world through Him might be saved." Jesus didn't come for condemnation and destruction. He came to bring good news—salvation, deliverance, forgiveness, and healing.

I read letters, books, and commentaries, and I talk with a lot of people who think God is the author of the bad things that have happened in this planet. If He is not the author, they think *He is the One who has given permission to the enemy to do these things.*

I want to assure you, *God is not giving the devil permission to do evil things.* You need to get that kind of thinking out of your mind. God and the devil are not working together to develop your character. The devil rebelled against God. He is a liar, a thief, and a murderer. Why would your Father use a liar, a thief, and a murderer to develop your character? Wake up! People have made that accusation against God many times. God is not your problem!

When God made man, He gave man dominion over the earth (see Gen. 1:26). That dominion is for a specific time frame. We know from the Book of Revelation that the time will come to an end, since one day Jesus will rule and reign over the entire world from Jerusalem.

In Genesis 3, when man sinned by yielding to lucifer's temptations and disobeying God, satan seized the dominion and authority from Adam and Eve in that moment. This is why satan is referred to as the god of this world in Second Corinthians 4:4. Jesus said, "The ruler of this world is coming, and he has nothing in Me" (John 14:30). There was a recognition of what satan had seized.

All the evil that has ever happened on this earth came from the fall of satan from his place as an archangel of God (lucifer), and from the fall of Adam and Eve in the Garden. Those two events opened the door for sin and death to pass upon the whole human race. The trail of tears of human history goes back to this point. This is where sickness, disease, wars, fighting, strife, child abuse, and every evil thing originated.

God gave the angels and mankind free will, and free will or choice is the essence of love. Without choice, you cannot love. You may wonder, *Why would God make a man who could choose to serve Him or reject Him?* When you serve God and love Him, He knows you chose to do it. You are not a robot. What pleasure would it bring to God if you were forced to love and serve Him?

People's bad choices have resulted in terrible problems. When you compound this over a period of 6,000 years, you have countless problems in the earth today. Disease and genetic mutations and all types of issues have happened in the human body. When God made planet Earth, it was all good. He did not put tornadoes in the Garden of Eden to wipe out Adam and Eve.

The fall of lucifer and the fall of man affected our planet. One day there is going to be a renovation of the planet. But right now, there are things that are in the earth and in the human race that are a result of the fall.

Your faith can change your world.

In addition, we see mistakes and sins come from human beings. A mistake is doing something that is wrong and that causes great difficulties. If you had known something was a mistake before you did it, you wouldn't have done it. A sin is a disobedient act against God. Other people may have made mistakes and sins, and we have made mistakes and sins that have all affected us.

So, when you look at what has happened, don't blame God. There are several other alternatives as to the cause of disaster, calamity, tragedy, destruction, stealing, killing, and all those bad things.

We know the original source of these things, and it has many branches as it goes through history and through life. Today we have people who have resigned themselves to saying, "*Que sera sera;* whatever will be will be." That's fatalism. This kind of believing says, "We have no control over anything. Our lives are like a piece of straw on the ocean. If something bad happens, or calamity or tragedy comes our way, that's just the way it is."

Then people jump to the next conclusion. Whatever your situation is right now and whatever is going to happen, it must be from God.

However, Your faith can change your world. Your belief in God can bring the good things of the Lord to you and stop the bad things of the devil from coming at your life.

JESUS PROCLAIMED GOOD NEWS

This is why Jesus came proclaiming good news:

The Spirit of the Lord is upon Me, because He has anointed Me to preach the gospel to the poor; He has sent Me to heal the brokenhearted, to proclaim liberty to the captives and recovery of sight to the blind, to set at liberty those who are oppressed (Luke 4:18).

"The Spirit of the Lord is upon Me, because He has anointed Me to preach the gospel to the poor...." His good news to the poor is: you don't have to stay in poverty anymore. Jesus went on to say, "He [God] has sent Me to heal the brokenhearted...." That's not *que sera sera*. That's not, "You have to live with a broken heart for the rest of your life." That's getting your broken heart healed.

Jesus was anointed "to proclaim liberty to the captives...." This is experiencing freedom and changing your destiny. "And recovery of sight to the blind...." This means sickness and disease can be reversed, and in their place you can have wholeness and health.

"To set at liberty those who are oppressed." Jesus will deliver you from all oppression.

We talked about Job earlier, but sometimes people think that God just turned Job over to the devil. But satan said to God, "Have You not made a hedge around him, around his household, and around all that he has on every side?" (Job 1:10).

It is *faith* that brings a hedge up around our lives, and it is *fear* that brings a hedge down. Faith and fear are opposites. Job was a righteous man. We should follow his example of upright-ness, but we should also remember this all-important fact: **Job did not have the New Covenant with the blood of Jesus Christ that we have today.** Today we can say, "God has redeemed us from the hand of the enemy." This was not possible when Job lived, because Jesus had not been cru-cified, buried, and resurrected yet.

> *It is faith that brings a hedge up around our lives, and it is fear that brings a hedge down.*

The most important thing that we can grasp is this: even though Adam lost dominion to satan, Jesus suffered for our sins, took our sicknesses, and took God's judgment for our sin, and on the third day He arose from the dead; when Jesus was raised up, He took the keys of authority from satan. Jesus disarmed all of the devil's might and dominion and arose victorious! He delivered us out from satan's authority, and the devil has no authority over us any-more. Today we are living under a New Covenant relationship (see Col. 2:14-15; Heb. 2:14).

Jesus freed us from satan's dominion by His love and His great mercy. It is vital that we understand that God is for us and He is on our side.

TRUTHS TO UNDERSTANDING SOVEREIGNTY

The word *sovereign* means "one possessing supreme authority and power." So "*Sovereignty*" means is the ultimate power, the supreme authority wielded by the predominant One—whatever. That's God. He is sovereign.

Here are three truths that will help you clearly understand the sovereignty of God:

1. *God has sovereignly revealed who He is, His nature and His character, in the Word of God.*

2. *God has sovereignly revealed His will in His Word.*

3. *God has revealed His principles or His ways in His Word.*

So we know God's nature, His will, His principles, and how He operates. Jesus taught the principle of sowing and reaping as He compared the Kingdom of Heaven to a farmer planting seed: first the blade develops, then the ear, then the full corn in the ear.

God gave a lease to Adam and Eve, and they lost their authority and dominion to satan who seized it. Then Jesus regained it through His death, burial, and resurrection. If you do not understand the importance of what Jesus did, then the devil will lie to you and you will be held by his deception. Even though he has no authority, he deceives people into thinking he does.

Faith believes, receives, speaks, and acts upon truth.

Some people doubt or waver in their belief that Jesus regained dominion and authority, and that He gives it to us when we accept Him as Savior and Lord of our lives. Other people know it and believe it, but they don't act on it. If you know something and believe it, but you don't act on it, you are still in a position of ineffectiveness in your faith. Faith believes, receives, speaks, and acts upon truth. It is this truth that will set you free, for Jesus said, "If you abide in My word, you are My disciples indeed. And you shall know the truth, and the truth shall make you free" (John 8:31-32).

GOD'S NATURE IN OPPOSITION TO SATAN'S NATURE

It is critical that we understand the nature of God and the nature of the devil because first of all, we need to *finish our race strong*. We don't want anyone to get on an early bus to go to Heaven. We love Heaven and we are going there one day, but we are not getting up a load right now.

There is a course to run, a faith to keep, a job to be completed. It is appointed to man once to die, but accidents and destruction, calamity, disaster, and disease are not the way God planned for people to leave. There have been people who chose martyrdom. Both Peter and Paul chose that route.

Second, it is important to know the nature of God and the nature of the devil because *you have loved ones who need your faith.* If you thought the problems, difficulties, calamities, and tragedies have come from God in the past, then what happens tomorrow if another attack comes against a family member? If you thought the last attack came from God, how can you pray this one off of the family member that you are praying for?

This is where some people have simply resigned themselves in almost a religious fatalism. They call it trust, but it's a fatalistic viewpoint. They are saying, "This is it. God is sovereign. He is all powerful and whatever happens must be from God."

All the bad things that have happened to you did not come from God. I would not accuse your father of it, so don't accuse my Father of it!

LET'S SET THE RECORD STRAIGHT!

Here are a few facts to set the record straight regarding God's sovereignty:

1. **God will not change His character, His nature, or who He is.**

   God is not good one day and bad the next. This is how some people have interpreted the word *sovereign*. "Well, since God is all powerful, He can do what He wants." He cannot and will not change His nature. He is love. He doesn't suddenly change who He is.

2. ***God will not violate His Word.***

   There are people who have taken the concept of being sovereign as if God could say one thing one day and the next day change it. Remember, God said, "For I am the Lord, I do not change..." (Mal. 3:6).

3. ***God will not violate His own principles, His nature, His will, or His Word.***

   What does this mean to you and me? It means we can put absolute confidence in the nature of God and in His Word. You can lock your faith into His Word and not get stabbed in the back. The perception some people have had is, "Well, I tried to believe, but then God came around the backside and did this bad thing." They back away from faith, which means they back away from standing on the Word of God.

   If you don't know why something happened and you can't explain it, at least don't blame God! Just be honest with God: "I don't know why this happened, but one thing I know is that You are a good God, You love me, and You are on my side. Whatever I missed or didn't do right, whatever I didn't know or whatever I could have done, show me."

   That is not heaping guilt on us or pointing the finger at any other person. It is simply saying, "I refuse to put guilt on God." It is vital for your future and for the future of your loved ones, because it is God who is going to bring you through to victory personally and help you bring victory to your loved ones.

4. ***God is good and He loves you with an eternal love.***

   That is His nature, and His mercy endures forever.

5. *There is an appointed time to die for every person.*

We know that from Hebrews 9:27: "It is appointed for men to die once, but after this the judgment."

There is coming a time for God's final judgment against sin. Right now we are walking in a place of mercy. We should be thankful for God's mercy, because if James and John had their way, we would already have been roasted and toasted! This is how some people think: "One strike and you are out of here. They didn't receive You, Jesus, so let's get rid of them."

So what happens when someone sins or they go away from God? God's Spirit is still dealing with them and working with them. Maybe you were a tough nut to crack and it took a long time for you to be saved and there were still things hanging on you when you got saved!

God receives us at death, but He is not out snatching people up! In John 14:3, Jesus said, "If I go and prepare a place for you, I will come again and receive you to Myself; that where I am, there you may be also."

There is a huge difference between God receiving someone who dies and snatching people up. That's the concept some people have had. "God took them." Or, "God picked that flower because He needed him or her up in Heaven to make His bouquet complete!" It is amazing the distorted concepts people have come up with.

God receives us, and Psalm 116:15 says, "Precious in the sight of the Lord is the death of His saints." Why would God call you and anoint you for a purpose on this earth, then take you out prematurely before that purpose is fulfilled? It is not His nature and it is against His purpose and plan.

God has a specific plan for each person, and He wants it completed, because there are people you will touch that no one else can reach. There are no lost people in Heaven to witness to. There are no sick people waiting to be healed. There are no people bound waiting to be delivered. That work is to be done here in the earth.

6. **God works all things together for good to those who love Him and to those who are called according to His purpose** (Rom. 8:28).

Personally Challenged, But Never Blamed God!

I think it is important for me to share with you that we have had some bad things happen in our lives, but we have never blamed God. We have gone through some accidents. The good news is, we are all alive and the repairs have been made. We have gone through sickness. Personally, I have gone through it. The good news is, we knew God did not send it and we believed that He would heal us. I am grateful that we are the healed of the Lord.

We have gone through difficulties—like having our house burn down in the middle of the night. We all escaped in our pajamas. We weren't checking to see what we could carry out with us as fire consumed the entire house within minutes.

I remember Sharon and I and our four children huddled on the front porch of the Browns, our neighbors across the street, after we had awakened them at 1:30 to 2:00 in the morning to call the Fire Department. In tears we praised God as we watched our house burn, not because it was burning, but because we weren't in there! We were alive and we had each other.

Why do I share this? We look back and say, "These things didn't come from God, but the restoration, the deliverance, and the preservation did come from God. God worked good out of these things."

Our perspective stays in the future: "Lord, help us in the days ahead to prevent these things from happening." But we also know, "Lord, You are going to work everything together for our good." God can turn it and work it for our good because our faith and trust are in Him.

DAUGHTER OF ABRAHAM DELIVERED

In Luke, chapter 13, there is a great story that clearly illustrates how God's goodness and His unchanging nature can change a bad situation for a person of covenant.

Jesus went into the synagogue and there was a woman who had been bent over for 18 years with an infirmity. Every day she looked at the ground because she couldn't look up. Jesus said to her, "Woman, you are loosed from your infirmity" (Luke 13:12). Then following verses tell of her deliverance and the resulting ruckus among the religious ruler and the crowd because Jesus healed her on the Sabbath:

And He [Jesus] *laid His hands on her, and immediately she was made straight, and glorified God.* [This woman had spent 18 years in a terrible condition of sickness and disease.]

But the ruler of the synagogue answered with indignation, because Jesus had healed on the Sabbath; and he said to the crowd, "There are six days on which men ought to work; therefore come and be healed on them, and not on the Sabbath day."

The Lord then answered him and said, "Hypocrite! Does not each one of you on the Sabbath loose his ox or donkey from the stall, and lead it away to water it?" (Luke 13:13-15).

In other words, they had more compassion for an animal than for a human being! They had missed the point of the Sabbath. It was not the day of the week that was important. It was the One we honor on that day and should honor every day of the week! Then Jesus said, "So ought not this woman, being a daughter of Abraham, *whom Satan has bound...*" (Luke 13:16).

Notice, Jesus cleared the air. God didn't send the sickness on this woman. He was not the cause. God didn't give the devil permission to afflict her. Her sickness was from an enemy (satan) who is loose on the planet.

When Jesus took the authority from satan, He did not annihilate the devil. Satan still is loose. Why? There is a time frame, a lease on the earth that God gave to man. Until that lease expires, the enemy is loose. God works everything on His time. There is coming a day when the devil will be bound, and there is a time coming when he will be cast into the lake of fire. Until that time, the devil is loose in the earth, *but he can be stopped and he can be resisted.*

Our own mistakes can be corrected. Our own sins can be repented of. Our own lack of knowledge can be corrected with right knowledge. Instead of looking back and finding fault with someone else, just say, "Lord, help me in the future."

"So ought not this woman, being a daughter of Abraham, whom Satan has bound—think of it—for eighteen years, be loosed from this bond on the Sabbath?" (Luke 13:16)

God had made a promise to Abraham: "Blessing I will bless you, and multiplying I will multiply your descendants as the stars of the heaven and as the sand which is on the seashore..." (Gen. 22:17). This woman was a direct descendant of Abraham. Everything God said to Abraham, He was saying to her.

Part of that was, "I will be your God." That means, "I will be your Provider, Healer, Deliverer, Rescuer, and Savior. Whatever you have need of I AM." This is why God revealed Himself to Moses as, "I AM WHO I AM...Thus you shall say to the children of Israel, 'I AM has sent me to you'" (Exod. 3:14). In other words, God was saying, "I AM whatever you need. I AM your source. I AM your peace. I AM your strength. I AM the way, the truth, and the life."

The woman with the spirit of infirmity for 18 years was a daughter of Abraham. She was under the Old Covenant, yet Jesus said, "Ought not this woman, being a daughter of Abraham...be loosed...?" (Luke 13:16).

You and I have a better covenant. Everything God promised to Abraham and his seed is in the New Covenant, plus a whole lot more. Under the Old Covenant, you could never be born again. You could never be the righteousness of God. You could never have the indwelling presence of God. Not only do we have the same God this woman had—the God who heals, delivers, and sets free in every area—but we have a God who indwells us by His presence. I am saying you ought to be healed and redeemed, because God loves you and cares for you! You are the seed of Abraham through your faith in Christ and you are an heir to the promises God made to him and his seed (see Gal. 3:13-14;26-29).

CHAPTER 6

THE FREE WILL OF MAN

In order to fully grasp and understand the issue that God is not your problem, we need to define "free will" or the power of choice.

"Free will" is being able to choose what you are going to do and which way you are going to go. It is deciding whether you will love God or reject Him, worship Him or not, give to His work or not, serve Him or not, or pray or not pray.

Every time we see an invitation for salvation given in Scripture, it is always related to "whoever will." In other words, a person has a choice to respond or not. "Whoever desires, let him take the water of life freely" (Rev. 22:17). "Whoever calls on the name of the Lord shall be saved" (Rom. 10:13).

God set the example of free will. John 3:16 says, "For God so loved the world that He gave His only begotten Son...." God did not have to give His Son. He chose to give Him. Jesus gave His life for us on the cross. He was not forced to give it. He chose to give His life. So God the Father, God the Son, and God the Holy Spirit all have free will or choice. It is part of God's makeup.

Why does God give freedom of choice? It is the essence of love. Without the ability to choose, you cannot love. Love is rooted in choice. So when you worship God, He knows you are not faking it. A person can be lifting his hands or singing, but when a person truly worships from his heart, God knows it. When someone truly loves God from his heart, He knows it. Why? He doesn't make anyone do it.

It is the same way between two people. Without choice there is no love. Someone may force you to do something, but they cannot force you to love. Love is always rooted in choice.

God gave choice or freedom of will to satan. He was once the archangel, lucifer, who led worship. Also, we know that God gave freedom of choice to the other angels because when lucifer chose to rebel and go his own way, one-third of the angels made the same choice.

One thing angels don't have that you and I have is redemption. You should thank God that you have redemption because with lucifer, and the angels who decided to rebel with him, it was one strike and you're out.

In Luke 10:18, Jesus said, "I saw Satan fall like lightning from heaven." Lucifer's relationship with God was over for eternity. He would be separated from God forever.

God gave free will and free choice to Adam and Eve. They had the choice to honor God, to love Him, to respond to Him, to obey Him, and to fellowship with Him, but they chose to disobey God and obey satan's words. "Choice" opened the door for the whole human race to have sin and death come upon them. God has given freedom of choice to every human being who has ever lived. The phrase, "God allowed it," spins off of this.

"GOD ALLOWED IT"

I want to give you a couple of scenarios. Satan sold out and rebelled against God and led one-third of the angels in rebellion with him. Did it really happen? Yes. Did God want it? No. Was it God's best? No. Was it God's will? No. Just because something is allowed does not mean it is God's will, God's choice, or God's best. It is very important that we understand this, because sometimes when we use the phrase, "God allowed it," it is as if we are saying, "God willed it, planned it, and prepared it."

Adam and Eve rejected God's commands and chose satan's command and opened the whole human race up to sin and death. Did God allow it? Yes. Was it God's will? No, it was not God's will, and it wasn't God's best. It was not God's choice for them.

When we use the phrase, "God allowed it," it does not mean that God chose it, that He willed it, or that He directed it. As we look across the earth, let me ask you, does God allow wars? Yes. Does He allow disease? Yes. Does He allow broken marriages and homes and families? Yes. Abuse? Yes. *Does God will it? No!*

This is what we must understand, because so many people are alienated from God over this. They say, "Well, if God is who He is, then why does He allow all of these things to happen?" *It is because God gave man free will.* God gave man freedom of choice. Sickness, disease, wars, calamities, and tragedies are allowed in the earth, but *they are not God's will, His plan, or His best.*

Jesus' Life: The Greatest Revelation of the Will of God

What is God's will? How do we know it? The greatest revelation of the will of God is in His Son Jesus Christ. He was the Word made flesh. In John 14:9, Jesus said, "He who has seen Me has seen the Father...." Jesus said that He was in His Father and His Father was in Him. If you want to know the will of God, look at Jesus and read His words. *The will of God is made up of what He said and what He did.*

Let me ask you a few more questions:

Q: How many people did Jesus make sick?

A: None.

Q: How many people did Jesus cause to have accidents and calamities while He was on the earth?

A: None.

Q: How many people did Jesus kill before it was their time to die?

A: None.

Then, why does God get blamed for causing sickness, calamities, and premature death as if He wanted it to happen? We can look at how it was before Adam and Eve sinned in the Garden and find out God's will. Everything was good. Then, how is it going to be when we are in Heaven? There will be no sickness, no disease, no calamity, and no tragedy.

The very clear representation of God's will is the Son, Jesus Christ. He revealed that God is a good God and that He loves us. Instead of sinking the disciples in the lake, Jesus saved them from the storm. The way many people have it, they would have said, "God sent the storm to teach them a lesson." Wake up!

Let's look at John 10:11 again where Jesus said, "I am the good shepherd. The good shepherd gives His life for the sheep." He doesn't lay His life down for the sheep and then cut off their ears! How many times have people given misinformation about God, about His character, and about His nature? He is good all the time. His nature is unchanging.

> *If you want to know the will of God, look at Jesus and read His words.*

MISINFORMATION: SATAN'S TOOL

One of the greatest tools of warfare strategy is misinformation. The attack on Pearl Harbor was a success from the Japanese standpoint because of misinformation. They had sent so many signals, directives, and pieces of false information that our military was not in a state of preparedness.

When you think of D-Day and the invasion of Normandy at the end of World War II; one of the reasons the allies were able to penetrate so quickly into France was because of misinformation. The German army's top leadership did not know where the invasion was going to happen. There was misinformation that possibly we were going to send the main invasion force to another location. The German troops were scattered and held in position until enough time had lapsed that we were able to establish a beachhead and advance across France, then on into the rest of Europe.

The devil understands misinformation and he understands warfare. One of his greatest tools has been misinforming people about God's character and nature.

One of the most important reasons for you to be established in your understanding of the nature and character of God is that if you think God sent a sickness or a disease, calamity or tragedy, upon one of your loved ones in days gone by, what happens if one of your loved ones is faced with a similar situation again? If you think God sent the last situation, you will have no faith to pray for this one. Why? How can you pray for God to remove something that you think He sent? If you think He sent it, even if He did remove it, how long do you think He has to keep it there before removing it? This is where many people have no faith in their prayer life. They have no confidence. They have moved into a fatalistic viewpoint, and that is, "Whatever will be will be. Whatever happens, it must be God."

Once you understand free will, then you will understand why bad things happen on the earth, even though God is still supreme. Man has had free choice for 6,000 years to do right or wrong, and a lot of wrong has happened. It has been compounded and multiplied and it has affected many people. However, it has not changed the supreme power of God.

When God said, "I give you dominion," that was for a specific time period in the earth. Revelation tells us there is a day coming when that time will be up and Jesus will rule and reign once again. But until that time, God has given man dominion on the earth.

AVOIDING ERRONEOUS PERCEPTIONS OF GOD

As I shared in the previous chapter, God is sovereign. He sovereignly spoke His will and revealed His Word. In supreme power He spoke His ways and His principles and revealed who He is. He sovereignly revealed His character. He is Jehovah Jireh, the Provider. He is Jehovah Rapha, the Healer. Just because God is sovereign does not mean that He will suddenly turn around and change and be a different God from one day to the next. This is where the teaching on sovereignty has been in error. People have said, "Well, since God is sovereign, He can do anything He wants."

This is not true, for God cannot change His Word and He cannot change His character. He is forever the same, and what He has spoken in His Word will not change. You can lock your life into God's Word and He will fulfill it. He is not going to lie to you and turn around and say, "I didn't mean it!"

When some people teach on sovereignty, the whole concept you get is, "You never know what God is going to do." I am telling you, you *can know exactly what God is going to do.* He is going to perform His Word. He will honor His Word. He will live up to His character.

In every specific situation, God may choose different ways to do something and you may not know all the particulars. But you can be assured that He will fulfill His Word, He will honor His character, and He will honor the principles that He has established in the Word.

> *You can know exactly what God is going to do.*
>
> *He is going to perform His Word. He will honor His Word. He will live up to His character.*

God wants good things for you. I am amazed at people who will fight to stay sick. There are people who will argue tooth and toenail to stay in the place of accidents, calamities, and tragedies. I have never been able to comprehend that, and I say, "Show me in Scripture where Jesus brought any of those things on people." We see Jesus doing the opposite: saving people from calamity and from the storm, multiplying loaves and fishes, and casting demons out of people.

GOD IS FOR YOU!

In Romans 8:31-32, Paul said:

What then shall we say to these things? If God is for us, who can be against us?

He who did not spare His own Son, but delivered Him up for us all, how shall He not with Him also freely give us all things?

God went beyond all limits. He gave the best that He had. If God gave the best that He had, why would He withhold anything of lesser value from you? He gave His Son, Jesus Christ. With Him He freely gives us all things.

God is the Prince of Peace, not the prince of torment. He is the Healer, not the one who makes people sick. In Exodus 15:26, He says, "I am the Lord who heals you." He is Jehovah Jireh, the God who sees ahead and makes provision, not the one who sends poverty and lack. He does not change His character. He loves you with an everlasting love.

I want to encourage you, if the Lord is on your side, why don't you get on His side? *Why accuse God of being your problem when He is the answer?* Why have a suspicion about His character that He may be behind your troubles when Jesus gave His blood on the cross to pay for your sins? That's pretty low to be suspicious about the One who gave every drop of His blood for you, thinking He is behind all of your problems, difficulties, calamities, tragedies, and all the bad things that have happened.

Jesus poured out His blood and took the stripes on His back to redeem you and me from the curse.

To me we are talking about a bigger issue than many people realize. With this in mind, let's look at Romans 8:31-34:

If God is for us, who can be against us?

He who did not spare His own Son, but delivered Him up for us all, how shall He not with Him also freely give us all things?

Who shall bring a charge against God's elect? It is God who justifies [declares not guilty].

Who is he who condemns? It is Christ who died, and furthermore is also risen, who is even at the right hand of God, who also makes intercession for us.

God is not praying against you. He is praying for you. Some people's concept is, "God is going to get you." I've got a word for you: **God is going to bless you!**

Why accuse God of being your problem when He is the answer?

Many people won't go to church because at some point of difficulty in their life they were told, "God let you down." "God didn't come through." "God was responsible for that car accident." "God allowed it." I am telling you, if we can get the misinformation out of people's minds, Jesus will be irresistible. He is the most wonderful Savior.

We need to clear all the negative labels that have been put on Him and all the fog that has been around His personhood. He is unchanging. The enemy understands warfare, and his goal is to keep people separated from a loving God. Misinformation is one of the best ways to do that, for if people are misinformed about the character of God, they won't be drawn to Him.

This is why the Bible is called "the gospel"—the good news! Sometimes people become proclaimers of bad news: "Well, you know, the Lord might do this terrible thing to you. This bad thing happened because of God and that bad thing happened because of God. Do you want to be saved?"

Wake up! Why would people respond to that type of message?

Let's continue in Romans, chapter 8:

Who shall separate us from the love of Christ? Shall tribulation, or distress, or persecution, or famine, or nakedness, or peril, or sword?

As it is written: "For Your sake we are killed all day long; we are accounted as sheep for the slaughter" (Romans 8:35-36).

There *is* going to be persecution for righteousness' sake (see 2 Tim. 3:12). Paul talked about persecution and he experienced plenty of it! What I want to point out is, *persecution is not coming from God.* Paul faced the peril and the sword, but what was God's response to him? "My grace is sufficient for you…" (2 Cor. 12:9). We find Paul's response in Romans 8:37-39:

Yet in all these things we are more than conquerors through Him who loved us.

For I am persuaded that neither death nor life, nor angels nor principalities nor powers, nor things present nor things to come,

Nor height nor depth, nor any other created thing, shall be able to separate us from the love of God which is in Christ Jesus our Lord.

Sometimes people talk about suffering for Jesus, but often it is not a biblical suffering. It is in their minds that they are suffering. Why did the disciples suffer? They preached the gospel, they healed the sick, and they cast out devils. It wasn't just that they had overeaten and lain on the couch so long and watched so much TV that they were being persecuted! It was because they were out on the streets lifting up the name of Jesus Christ, telling of His love, getting the sick healed, and getting the devils cast out of people. Then persecution came. If you do the right things, you too will face persecution.

Persecution is not coming from God.

What some people label "persecution" has absolutely nothing to do with biblical persecution. It is their own fault, from their own lack of knowledge, or their own mistakes and what is going on in the earth.

It is true that in some parts of the earth Christians are facing persecution for their faith. We honor those who are living for Christ in dangerous places.

SIN CAN OPEN THE DOOR TO SICKNESS AND DISEASE

What about the consequences of sin? Does sin cause bad things to happen?

In John 5, Jesus went down to the pool of Bethesda and preached. There was a man there who had an infirmity for 38 years. He could not walk. When an angel went down into the pool and stirred the water, the first person in the water was healed. But this man could never make it in first because he had no one to help him.

Jesus said to him, "Rise, take up your bed and walk."

And immediately the man was made well, took up his bed, and walked. And that day was the Sabbath.

The Jews therefore said to him who was cured, "It is the Sabbath; it is not lawful for you to carry your bed." [They had no concern or joy over the man being healed, but they were bothered by that mattress he was carrying around!]

He answered them, "He who made me well said to me, 'Take up your bed and walk.'"

Then they asked him, "Who is the Man who said to you, 'Take up your bed and walk'?"

But the one who was healed did not know who it was, for Jesus had withdrawn, a multitude being in that place.

Afterward Jesus found him in the temple, and said to him, "See, you have been made well. Sin no more, lest a worse thing come upon you" (John 5:8-14).

> ## *Sin can open the door to sickness and disease.*

This word from Jesus tells us something. *Sin can open the door to sickness and disease.* Now, it does not say that every time someone is sick that sin is the cause. It is important that we don't read into it something that is not there. We know that sin may not be the cause of sickness in every situation. It's not sin that causes an innocent little baby to be sick. We know that when Adam and Eve sinned, they opened the door for sin and sickness to pass upon the entire human race. So there may be generations of effects that have happened in the genes of people that affect innocent children.

This passage also tells us that Jesus did not bring the sickness. *He brought the cure.* It is very important that we separate the two.

A lack of knowledge can open the door to the enemy, and there are principalities and powers at work in the world to bring evil upon people. But the good news is, you can stand against the works of the enemy. Once you know that God is on your side, you can also be assured that He has the answers for everything you will ever face!

> ## *Jesus did not bring the sickness. He brought the cure.*

CHAPTER 7

A CLOSER LOOK AT "WHY" BAD THINGS HAPPEN

Many people in the world today are asking, "If God is good all the time, then why do bad things happen? Where do the bad things come from? Why do they happen to good people?" Scripture gives us some clear-cut answers to these questions. We have already touched on this topic, but let's look in more depth at the causes as to why bad things happen.

GOD IS GOOD—THE DEVIL IS EVIL

God is a good God, and His will for your life is good. In Luke 12:32, Jesus says, "It is your Father's good pleasure to give you the kingdom." Then, in Third John 1:2, God makes it very clear that His will is that you would prosper: "Beloved, I pray that you may prosper in all things and be in health, just as your soul prospers." In other words, it is God's will that you prosper inwardly as well as outwardly.

> *God is a good God, and His will for your life is good.*

In Deuteronomy, chapter 28, you can see clearly that it is God's will to prosper you—if you obey you will be blessed, if you disobey you will be cursed. In Deuteronomy 30:19, God says, "I have set before you life and death, blessing and cursing; therefore *choose life*, that both you and your descendants may live."

When God created the world and mankind He said, "Then God saw everything that He had made, and indeed it was *very good…*" (Gen. 1:31).

If we look at the end of the Book, Revelation 21:1-5, we find out that in the end everything is *very good*:

> *Now I saw a new heaven and a new earth, for the first heaven and the first earth had passed away. Also there was no more sea.*
>
> *Then I, John, saw the holy city, New Jerusalem, coming down out of heaven from God, prepared as a bride adorned for her husband.*
>
> *And I heard a loud voice from heaven saying, "Behold, the tabernacle of God is with men, and He will dwell with them, and they shall be His people. God Himself will be with them and be their God.*
>
> *"And God will wipe away every tear from their eyes; there shall be no more death, nor sorrow, nor crying. There shall be no more pain, for the former things have passed away."*
>
> *Then He who sat on the throne said, "Behold, I make all things new."*

It was good in the beginning and it is good in the ending. So what happened to cause the bad things to come in the middle—in our lives now? The answer is in the revelation understanding of what took place when Adam and Eve sinned.

To get a clear picture of what happened spiritually, let's look at Romans 5:12: "Through one man sin entered the world, and death through sin, and thus death spread to all men, because all sinned."

Paul had the revelation that when Adam and Eve sinned and they were driven from the garden, *their sin opened the door for sin and death to pass onto the entire human race.* They had the keys of authority and dominion, but when they sinned the devil took those keys.

The one you obey becomes your master. When they obeyed the devil's voice instead of God's voice, they surrendered to a different master. As a result, dominion and authority were taken from them.

This explains why, after Jesus had been crucified, buried, and resurrected, He announced, "All authority has been given to Me in heaven and on earth" (Matt. 28:18). "I am He that liveth and was dead; and, behold, I am alive for evermore, Amen; and have the keys of hell and of death" (Rev. 1:18 KJV). These keys represent *authority*. Jesus regained the authority and dominion that Adam and Eve lost.

When you give someone the key to a city or to a state, it represents authority. The devil had accomplished something evil by deceiving Adam and Eve into sin and seizing those keys. But when Jesus rose from the dead, He crushed the authority of the devil and by His conquest, He seized the keys and led captivity captive. The righteous dead of the Old Testament who were kept in the bosom of Abraham, were led out of paradise by Jesus when He was raised and they were translated into Heaven. That's why the Old Testament saints who had died were seen alive on Jesus' resurrection day.

So when you grasp the picture of what happened, Adam and Eve opened the door to all evil. A multitude of evils came upon the earth as a result of their sin.

Romans 5:15 gives us more insight: "But the free gift is not like the offense. For if by the one man's offense many died, much more the grace of God and the gift of the grace of the one Man, Jesus Christ, abounded to many."

Through Adam's sin, many came into spiritual death, but through one Man's obedience (that of Jesus Christ), many have found life. "And the gift is not like that which came through the one who sinned. For the judgment which came from one offense resulted in condemnation, but the free gift which came from many offenses resulted in justification" (Rom. 5:16).

Jesus' death on the cross and the giving of His life doesn't condemn us; it justifies us or declares us not guilty.

"For if by the one man's offense death reigned through the one…" (Rom. 5:17). Through Adam's sin, the law of sin and death seized power in the earth. God gave one man, Adam, the power to keep evil from happening, but instead of stopping the devil, he opened the door to him to come upon the entire human race. The history of the world is the story of satan's rule over the lives of men who did not know God or how to stop the devil.

That's why there was such a cry for a Deliverer to come. Even in this hour, though people have religion, many don't know Jesus and they are still being slaughtered or run over by the enemy.

Adam's sin caused death to reign, but here's the flip side of it. "Much more those who receive abundance of grace and of the gift of righteousness will reign in life through the One, Jesus Christ" (Rom. 5:17). If you receive Jesus Christ as your Lord and Savior, you can reign *in this life.* Instead of sin and death ruling your life, righteousness and grace will rule in your family, in your home, and in your mind.

SUMMARY OF REASONS WHY BAD THINGS HAPPEN

Here is a summary of reasons why bad things happen to good people.

1. *The covering archangel, lucifer, sinned.* (See Isaiah 14:12-14 and; Ezekiel 28:12-15.)

2. *The devil caused Adam and Eve to sin.*

    The first two people who had dominion in the earth opened the door to the devil. Bad things can happen to innocent people, not necessarily because they have sinned, but because the law of sin and death is operating in disease, calamities, tragedies, and disasters.

3. *Bad things can happen because of our own sin.*

   Bad things happen to people at times because of their own sin. Usually, most people don't want to accept this reason.

   If someone consumes alcohol and gets behind the wheel of a car and has a car wreck because they are not under control, bad things can result in their own life as well as in the lives of other people. We know several people whose lives were taken because they overdosed on drugs or alcohol, or a combination of both.

   Sin has consequences. Proverbs 26:2 says, "A curse without cause shall not alight." In other words, there is always a cause when the curse pays a visit. We need to determine what it is. I am not trying to condemn anyone. If you have sinned, opening the door for bad things to come, repent and shut the door to the devil.

4. *Bad things happen because of the sin of other people.*

   A lot of bad things happen, not necessarily because someone has done something wrong, but because someone else has done something wrong. The sin of other people affects innocent people.

   Think about the innocent children in war-torn countries. What did they do to cause their mother and father to be shot and their home to be blown apart? The sin of other people affected them.

   Bad things are not the will of God but they are the result of the curse that was loosed in the earth when Adam and Eve sinned. Their fall opened the door to another element that many people do not realize and that is, nature itself is under a curse. God doesn't create good people just so a hurricane or a tornado can tear them up. There is a terrible misconception about all the innocent people who have died and lost their homes because of tornados or hurricanes. Many people call those phenomena: "acts of God." That wasn't an act of God. It is nature that is out of control.

Romans 8:22 says, "For we know that the whole creation groans and labors with birth pangs together until now." Things are happening in the human race and in the earth that God did not intend. Man's sin opened the door to it, and until satan's lease on the earth is up, those bad things will exist.

Before you think I'm saying that we are subject to all these bad things, the good news is, Jesus rebuked the storm and *He has given every bornagain believer authority to rebuke the storms that come against their life.*

Jesus was headed across the sea to deliver a demonpossessed man when a storm came up. His disciples said, "Teacher, do You not care that we are perishing?" (Mark 4:38). The storm was sent to stop them from reaching the other side, because the devil had control of the entire region of Gadara.

When Jesus stilled the storm, they went to the other side of the lake and the devil was cast out of that man. Jesus told this man, "Go home to your friends, and tell them what great things the Lord has done for you" (Mark 5:19). As a result of this man's deliverance, the entire region opened up to the gospel.

The enemy will try to bring natural things against you to stop you from achieving your purpose. If something bad happens to another person, don't be quick to judge them as having sinned. Other factors may be involved.

5. **Bad things happen because of the mistakes of other people.**

For instance, an air crash happened in Little Rock, Arkansas, because of someone's mistake. A thunderstorm hit the airport with wind gusts of over 80 miles an hour and the runway was wet. There was no way for the plane to stop, so it went off the runway and crashed. No one was trying to sin in that situation, and there is no reason that we should try to find fault or blame, but neither should we say, "Well, I guess that was God's will." It was *not* God's will.

God has given us His Word and His Spirit to help us avoid human error. The closer we walk in line with the principles of His Word and the more attention we give to the Holy Spirit's voice, we will avoid the disasters that result from human error.

A member of our congregation, Dr. Givens, came running up to me as I was giving the altar call at a Sunday morning service. His son was booked on the ValuJet flight out of Miami that crashed in the Everglades. He and his wife learned about the plane crash as they watched CNN.

For years the Givens family and another family had stood on God's Word and prayed divine protection over each other's children. They agreed in prayer that both they and their seed had been redeemed from the curse and that the angels of God would protect them.

Hours after the ValuJet crash, the Givens' son called and told them what had happened. He and a friend were at the counter near the jet way, ready to board the ValuJet when he said, "Something inside of me said, 'Don't get on that flight.'" He and his friend went over to the Fort Lauderdale Airport to catch another plane. Miraculously, they were delivered.

We should believe in order to hear God's voice so we will be delivered from human error. The lives of every person on board the ValuJet were snuffed out instantly when it crashed. As we are led by God's Spirit, protection and deliverance are available to us from tragedies, calamities, and destruction of any kind.

6. *Bad things happen as a result of the operation of demons in the earth.*

After the Columbine shootings in Littleton, Colorado, Dr. Billy Graham was asked on *Larry King Live*, "How do you explain this?" Billy Graham answered, "There are demons in the earth."

Things are happening that are not rational. What would cause someone to shoot their classmates? Why are students in public schools suddenly under attack? One of the reasons is because of the transmittal of evil and filth through TV, rock concerts, videos, and movies. People are receiving thoughts, ideas, and imaginations of the devil, then the enemy comes to fan the fire that has been planted on the inside of them. People act out what they have seen and heard.

7. *Bad things happen because of persecution for righteousness' sake.*

Paul preached in a city and cast the devil out of a girl who was bound by a fortune-telling spirit. Scripture says, "When her masters saw that their hope of profit was gone, they seized Paul and Silas and dragged them into the marketplace to the authorities" (Acts 16:19).

Verses 22 and 23 reveal what happened as a result of Paul doing good by setting the girl free from the fortune-telling spirit:

Then the multitude rose up together against them; and the magistrates tore off their clothes and commanded them to be beaten with rods.

And when they had laid many stripes on them, they threw them into prison, commanding the jailer to keep them securely.

Can you imagine Silas asking Paul, "Have you sinned?" or Paul saying to Silas, "You need to examine your heart, brother"?

Now, there are times when someone has done something wrong. We can see at times where nature was out of control and where there was a mistake or an error in human judgment. But at other times it is the work of the devil or persecution for righteousness' sake, which comes from the devil.

A missionary and his two small sons went to help at a missions station in India. They were camping inside of their utility vehicle. Suddenly they were surrounded by a band of Hindus who barricaded all the doors to the mission compound so no one could get out to help them. Then, they set fire to the truck and burned the man and his two sons alive. This happened while Sharon and I were preaching in India.

At this very hour, there are people whose lives are being taken because of unjust persecution for the gospel's sake.

In Hebrews, chapter 11, some people who were persecuted were miraculously delivered. Verse 35 says, "Others were tortured, not accepting deliverance, that they might obtain a better resurrection."

While some were cut in two, others were burned alive. Some were thrown into a pot of boiling oil. Other saints were thrown into a lions' den. Scripture says all of these saints—those who were delivered as well as those who were martyred—received a good report from God.

The important thing for us to realize is that when persecution comes against us, we should rejoice. Paul said, "The Lord will deliver me from every evil work and preserve me for His heavenly kingdom..." (2 Tim. 4:18).

Jesus talked about persecution in Matthew, chapter 5:

Blessed are those who are persecuted for righteousness' sake, for theirs is the kingdom of heaven.

Blessed are you when they revile and persecute you, and say all kinds of evil against you falsely for My sake.

Rejoice and be exceedingly glad, for great is your reward in heaven, for so they persecuted the prophets who were before you (Matthew 5:10-12).

It is important that we make a decision to clean up the things in our life personally that are not right. We should also make a decision that we will be strong in the Spirit to resist the attacks of the devil.

This is not an hour to take our relationship with Jesus lightly. Many people are halfhearted. They look at the bad things that are happening and say, "*Que sera sera.*" We need to understand that it is God's will for us to have life and have it more abundantly, and that it is God's will that we be delivered out of the hand of the enemy.

Ruling our own spirit as well as exercising the dominion and authority we have been given in Christ Jesus will effectively assist in keeping satan under our feet!

Ruling our own spirit as well as exercising the dominion and authority we have been given in Christ Jesus will effectively assist in keeping satan under our feet!

CHAPTER 8

RULING YOUR OWN SPIRIT

Often bad things that happen to people are simply the end result of their attitudes and actions. The bad things are not God's work. Recognize that you can change your own life personally and you can stop a lot of bad things from happening.

In the natural we tend to evaluate the "greatness" of people by their performance in music, sports, business, politics, or in any other area. But Proverbs 16:32 gives us a guideline for measuring or evaluating a person's "greatness": "He who is slow to anger is better than the mighty, and he who rules his spirit than he who takes a city."

According to this standard, a prime minister, a congressman, a president, or a CEO may not be considered great spiritually, nor army generals who have, in the natural, taken cities in feats of war such as: Alexander the Great, Charlemagne, Napoleon, Pershing from World War I, Schwarzkopf from Desert Storm, and others.

The Word of God is saying, "It is more difficult for a person to control their own spirit than it is for a general to conquer a city."

How many people do you know right now who are out of control in their spirit? What is the evidence that someone doesn't have control of their spirit? Strife or a foul mouth are two primary evidences.

The root cause of divorce is selfishness. Either one or both parties have no control of their spirit and they strike out with words and/or actions.

Why is there so much abuse in the world in this hour? People don't know how to rule their own spirit. It is unimaginable that someone would abuse an innocent baby, yet again and again the Department of Human Services is forced to take action to rescue babies. Sometimes they are too late and death is the result.

Many people look for a Band-Aid when they are unwilling to go to the root of the problem. The root cause of many bad things that happen is a person's refusal to control their own spirit—to rule their inner man.

You can shut the door on problems in your life if you will begin to rule on the inside. Many people want to rule the outside. They want to rule other people. They want to go to the top of the corporate ladder. They want to be number one in sports. But the biggest victory you will ever win *is the victory over your own spirit.* If you rule your own spirit and you are slow to anger, you are better than the mighty, stronger than someone who can take a city.

Proverbs 19:11 says, "The discretion of a man makes him slow to anger, and his glory is to overlook a transgression." *Discretion* is the ability to avoid thoughts, words, actions, and attitudes that can lead to undesirable consequences. A person with discretion has enough sense to know that if he or she gets involved in an ungodly relationship or partnership, trouble is ahead! Traps and snares are set to catch people who exercise no discretion.

The biggest victory you will ever win is the victory over your own spirit.

Discretion comes from meditating in God's Word and allowing the Holy

Spirit to speak into your life on a daily basis. He will warn you: "This is a wrong situation or a wrong circumstance. This is not the right direction." Discretion will lead you to change your course. You may have initiated some action, but suddenly you realize, that's the wrong way to go.

Proverbs 19:19 says, "A man of great wrath will suffer punishment; for if you rescue him, you will have to do it again." "A man of great wrath" is someone who has no control over his own spirit. He or she spouts off at the mouth anytime they want. Their idea of being free is saying whatever they want to say. Under the guise of being liberated, they have absolutely no control of their tongue.

Your mouth will put you under or it will put you over. "Death and life are in the power of the tongue…" (Prov. 18:21). It is important to set a guard over your lips, a watch over your mouth, so that what you say is in agreement with God's Word (see Ps. 141:3).

Every thought that crosses your mind is not necessarily a thought from God. The Bible says imaginations and thoughts that do not agree with God's Word are to be cast down:

Casting down imaginations, and every high thing that exalteth itself against the knowledge of God, and bringing into captivity every thought to the obedience of Christ. (2 Corinthians 10:5 KJV).

Wrong attitudes cause people to respond in anger and bitterness. We've had to deal with this in athletics with Christian teams. We have had to deal with it with parents who sit on the sidelines and if the referee calls a foul against their child, they are up off the bench, thinking it's their privilege to berate the man by screaming and yelling at him.

There are many people who need to lay an axe to the root of anger inside of their heart. Why? You cannot get the blessing of God by praising Him outwardly but having a lack of control of your spirit inwardly. An uncontrollable spirit will ruin and wreck marriages, homes, and families, and rob you of wonderful business deals.

The good news is, there is Someone who can control us and that is Jesus. I am talking about letting Jesus be the Lord of your life and letting Him rule you on the inside.

Sometimes people attribute their anger to what other people do. People who do not control their spirit will almost inevitably blame someone else. The abused child—whether the abuse is sexual, verbal, or physical—usually is made to believe that he or she is the cause of the abuse. Something he or she did or said triggered something in the father or mother, relative, or another person that made them abuse them. The child is hit not only with the pain and rejection of abuse, but with guilt and condemnation. There is a way to get free on the inside and that is to accept Jesus as Lord and Savior and with His help, bring your flesh under the control of the Holy Spirit.

People who are trying to get over the outward problems of alcohol, drugs, lying, stealing, and other things are dealing with a lack of control in their spirit.

In Second Timothy 3:1-4, Paul says that in the last days "perilous times will come"; then he goes on to say:

*For men will be lovers of themselves, lovers of money, boasters, proud, blasphemers, disobedient to parents, unthankful, unholy, unloving, unforgiving, slanderers, **without self-control**, brutal, despisers of good, traitors, headstrong, haughty, lovers of pleasure rather than lovers of God* (2 Timothy 3: 2-4).

Notice, "no self-control" is one attribute of people in the last days. In this hour, there are many people who are void of a conscience and out of control. In Galatians 5:23, "self-control" is listed as one of the nine fruits of the Holy Spirit. "Ruling your own spirit" and "having self-control" mean the same thing.

I was talking with a man recently who had been involved in a wrong relationship. I said to him, "You can't go back in that flesh relationship and expect to experience the blessings of God." I talked to him later and he said, "I broke it off."

When you start tearing flesh in breaking wrong relationships, there may be some sparks that fly. A heart decision determines what the flesh is going to do. In other words, your flesh may be what's involved, but the heart decided to yield to temptation.

James 1:19-20 says, "So then, my beloved brethren, let every man be swift to hear, slow to speak, slow to wrath; for the wrath of man does not produce the righteousness of God."

When someone's spirit is out of control, it will bring devastation. James has something to say about an uncontrolled spirit:

Where there is envy, strife, bitterness, and resentment, where someone has no control over their spirit, there will be confusion and every evil work.

> But if you have bitter envy and self-seeking [the King James Version says "strife"] in your hearts, do not boast and lie against the truth.
>
> This wisdom does not descend from above, but is earthly, sensual, demonic.
>
> For where envy and self-seeking [again the King James Version says "strife"] exist, confusion and every evil thing are there (James 3:14-16).

Where there is envy, strife, bitterness, and resentment, where someone has no control over their spirit, there will be confusion and every evil work.

Why do bad things happen? Sometimes people say, "We bound the devil and cast him out." They may have done all the right things outwardly, but if they have not dealt with their own spirit, there is an open door for the enemy.

What should you do if someone strikes at you? Let's look at the example Jesus gave us in First Peter 2:21-24:

For to this you were called, because Christ also suffered for us, leaving us an example, that you should follow His steps:

"Who committed no sin, nor was deceit found in His mouth";

who, when He was reviled, did not revile in return; when He suffered, He did not threaten, but committed Himself to Him who judges righteously;

who Himself bore our sins in His own body on the tree, that we, having died to sins, might live for righteousness—by whose stripes you were healed.

When Jesus was reviled, which means "subjected to verbal abuse," He did not revile in return. When He suffered, He didn't threaten or strike back. Scripture says He "committed Himself to Him who judges righteously" (1 Pet. 2:23).

When you commit your life into God's hands, you can say, "Lord, You take care of this situation. I can't handle it." When you commit situations into the Lord's hands—to the One who judges righteously—you will be amazed how He will turn situations around. He will give you favor, He will raise you up, and He will deliver you.

When Jesus was crucified, it looked like everything was over. It looked as if He had lost. But on the third day, He was vindicated in one moment. God has a resurrection day for each of us when we turn our situations to Him. He is *never* the source of evil or negative situations, but He is the Answer and has the divine strategy to overcome in *every situation.*

In a home and family, it's not enough just to say, "These are the rules and this is what we are going to do." We've got to work to bring everyone in that family to the point where Christ is

It is not by the law but by the cross that you have power over the enemy and you can control your flesh.

ruling their spirit, because when Jesus is ruling on the inside, the outward situations will be resolved.

It is not by the law but by the cross that you have power over the enemy and you can control your flesh.

In His flesh, Jesus did not want to go through Calvary, but in the garden of Gethsemane He said, "Father, if it is Your will, take this cup away from Me; nevertheless not My will, but Yours, be done" (Luke 22:42). Jesus ruled His own spirit even though He wanted to go another way.

By accepting the work of Jesus' death, burial, and resurrection, you can walk in freedom over every work of the enemy and live in the abundance that God has provided for you *in Christ*. No longer should there be any blaming God.

CHAPTER 9

SATAN'S "STINGER" HAS BEEN REMOVED

When you get a revelation of how God sees you, it will change you on the inside. No longer will you think of yourself as a worm or afraid! You will see the Lion of the Tribe of Judah roaring out of you! You will see yourself with dominion and authority. When you pray, you aren't just pitching prayers up, hoping God will catch them! You will begin to believe that you receive the moment you pray (see Mark 11:24).

With an attitude of a lack of dominion in your life, you can be defeated. Dominion and authority are for every redeemed child of God.

First John 3:8 says, "He who sins is of the devil, for the devil has sinned from the beginning. For this purpose the Son of God was manifested, *that He might destroy the works of the devil.*" To *destroy* means to loose, to sever, to break, to demolish, or to undo. The devil's dominion has been demolished. Now you can rise up and walk in dominion and authority.

Where there was sickness, now there is health. Where there was bondage, now there is freedom. Where there was sadness, now there is joy. Where there was confusion, now there is peace. Jesus came to get back what the devil had stolen. Jesus was victorious. Now it is a settled issue: *Your triumph has been won!*

Hebrews 2:14-15 says:

> *Inasmuch then as the children have partaken of flesh and blood, He Himself likewise shared in the same, that through death He might destroy him who had the power of death, that is, the devil, and release those who through fear of death were all their lifetime subject to bondage.*

Jesus became a human being to taste death for us. His shed blood freed us from satan's captivity. If the devil had known and understood God's plan, he never would have crucified Jesus; because once he crucified Him, Jesus broke the power of death. From that vantage point, He liberated us from the fear of dying. The grave cannot keep us, and death cannot hold us. For the born-again believer, death is like changing clothes.

When you get a revelation of how God sees you, it will change you on the inside.

I used to catch little bees with stingers on them. I would take the stinger out of the bees and let them crawl on my hand. When you take the stinger out and the bee crawls on you, it is nothing more than a roly-poly or a June bug crawling on your hand.

Jesus took the stinger out of the devil. Satan wants to make you think he has the power and authority, but he is a liar and the father of lies.

In Colossians 2:13-15, Paul is writing to his fellow believers in Colosse, telling them they have been forgiven, that all their sins that were against them and the penalty for them have been wiped away. He tells how Jesus disarmed satan and took his authority away from him. Let's look at these verses:

And you, being dead in your trespasses and the uncircumcision of your flesh, He has made alive together with Him, having forgiven you all trespasses. [That's every sin and every wrong thing. He made us alive and now we are born again, which means we have the life of Heaven in us. We are children of God.]

Having wiped out the handwriting of requirements that was against us, which was contrary to us. And He has taken it out of the way, having nailed it to the cross.

Having disarmed principalities and powers, He made a public spectacle of them, triumphing over them in it (Colossians 2:13-15).

Sin carries the penalty of death. You had notes against you for such things as lying, stealing, cheating, fear, lust, and anger. But Jesus took the handwriting of all the notes that were against you and He nailed them to the cross, marking your penalty for each of these notes "paid in full."

Paul gave the Colossians a graphic picture they could never forget. I pray you never forget it either! When satan, the accuser of the brethren, reminds you of what you did in the past and how you failed, turn his attention to the nail-scarred hands that paid *every note* you had against you.

When Jesus "disarmed principalities," He drew the stinger out of the principalities and powers. Ultimately, satan will be thrown in the lake of fire. Presently, he has been stripped of all of his authority, and the keys that he snatched from the first Adam were regained by the second Adam, Jesus Christ.

When this revelation gets inside of you, the old phrase, "The devil made me do it," will no longer be a part of your vocabulary. Instead of saying, "Whatever will be will be," begin to pray, "Lord, Your will be done on this earth as it is in Heaven." Begin to decree a thing, and God will establish it unto you.

Faith is the victory that overcomes the world. It is our faith in Jesus and what He did on the cross. In His death, burial, and resurrection, Jesus defeated satan and took the keys of authority from him. Now Jesus Christ reigns forever.

In Revelation 1:18 (KJV) Jesus said, "I am he that liveth, and was dead; and, behold, I am alive for evermore, Amen; and have the keys of hell and of death."

Satan does *not* have authority anymore. Whatever he had, Jesus took from him. Many evil things are still happening because people don't know this truth, or those who have heard it have yet to believe it, act upon it, and enforce it.

You can know the truth of satan's defeat and still be intimidated by him. It's time to rise up, take dominion, and declare and decree your victory: *The devil no longer rules in my life!*

NO LONGER INTIMIDATED BY SATAN

After Jesus' crucifixion, Mary Magdalene and the other Mary came to His tomb, but Jesus wasn't there. An angel spoke to them and said, "He is not here; for He is risen, as He said. Come, see the place where the Lord lay. And go quickly and tell His disciples that He is risen from the dead, and indeed He is going before you into Galilee; there you will see Him…" (Matt. 28:6-7).

Jesus appeared to the disciples and He said:

"All authority has been given to Me in heaven and on earth.

"Go therefore and make disciples of all the nations, baptizing them in the name of the Father and of the Son and of the Holy Spirit,

"teaching them to observe all things that I have commanded you; and lo, I am with you always, even to the end of the age." (Matthew 28:18-20).

In Mark 16:17-18, Jesus said:

"And these signs will follow those who believe: In My name they will cast out demons; they will speak with new tongues;

"they will take up serpents; and if they drink anything dead-ly, it will by no means hurt them; they will lay hands on the sick, and they will recover."

Peter and John were fishermen from Galilee. They had followed Jesus, and they had seen His miracles, but when they saw Him crucified, they ran in terror and hid. They were intimidated, ashamed, guilty, and taken captive with fear.

Then the day came in the upper room when the Holy Spirit came upon them. As they were flooded with the Spirit of God, suddenly they understood: *We are back in relationship with God. We have a New Covenant. Our sins are forgiven. We have the life of God in us. His resurrection is our resurrection. We have victory and triumph now because satan's "stinger" has been removed! The glory of God is back on us!*

Peter and John went to the temple to pray and instead of simply walking past the man who was "lame from his mother's womb...to ask alms from those who entered the temple" (Acts 3:2), Peter said, "In the name of Jesus Christ of Nazareth, rise up and walk" (Acts 3:6). Peter, a weak fisherman, spoke like a man with dominion, and power emanated from him. Scripture says:

And he [Peter] took him by the right hand and lifted him up, and immediately his feet and ankle bones received strength.

So he, leaping up, stood and walked and entered the temple with them—walking, leaping, and praising God (Acts 3:7-8).

It's time to rise up and use the authority you have been given in the name of Jesus. You exercise this authority with your words. It's time that you act like satan's stinger has been removed. He should be intimidated by you; you should not be intimidated by him!

When you combine your knowledge of satan's defeat with further understanding of the nature of God, you will realize that God had nothing to do with the bad things that happened to you in the past.

CHAPTER 10

ACCEPTANCE AND BENEFITS IN GOD'S FAMILY

In the story of the prodigal son in Luke 15, Jesus reveals the nature of the Father and His attitude toward His children. We are given a clear picture of what God wants for us, how He views us, and how we can respond to Him.

I'm sure you remember the story. The youngest of two sons came to his father and said, "Dad, I wish you were dead. I want my inheritance" (Luke 15:12, author's paraphrase). The father gave him his inheritance. Then, he left home and spent his inheritance on wild living. When he had nothing left, his friends departed, and he went to work for a pig farmer. With his face in a pigpen, he remembered how good things were back at Dad's house.

And he would gladly have filled his stomach with the pods that the swine ate, and no one gave him anything.

But when he came to himself, he said, "How many of my father's hired servants have bread enough and to spare, and I perish with hunger!

"I will arise and go to my father, and will say to him, 'Father, I have sinned against heaven and before you,

"'And I am no longer worthy to be called your son. Make me like one of your hired servants.'"

And he arose and came to his father. But when he was still a great way off, his father saw him and had compassion, and ran and fell on his neck and kissed him.

And the son said to him, "Father, I have sinned against heaven and in your sight, and am no longer worthy to be called your son."

But the father said to his servants, "Bring out the best robe and put it on him, and put a ring on his hand and sandals on his feet.

"And bring the fatted calf here and kill it, and let us eat and be merry;

For this my son was dead and is alive again; he was lost and is found." And they began to be merry" (Luke 15:16-24).

The elder brother heard the music and dancing. When he realized it was a celebration for his brother who had come home, he became angry. The elder brother said to his father:

"Lo, these many years I have been serving you; I never transgressed your commandment at any time; and yet you never gave me a young goat, that I might make merry with my friends.

"But as soon as this son of yours came, who has devoured your livelihood with harlots, you killed the fatted calf for him." (Luke 15:29-30).

The father's response to the elder son was:

*"Son, you are always with me, and **all that I have is yours.***

It was right that we should make merry and be glad, for your brother was dead and is alive again, and was lost and is found" (Luke 15:31-32).

God's message to you is the same: ***All that I have is yours!***

A CHEESE AND CRACKER DIET

I'm sure you have heard the story about an immigrant who was coming from Europe to America. When he bought his ticket and booked the passage on the ship, he brought a box of crackers and cheese with him so he would have food to eat while journeying to America. Each day he would eat a portion of his cheese and crackers.

As they neared the New York harbor, the captain said to him, "I noticed you never went into the dining area." Every day this guy had walked past the dining room and saw people eating from a wonderful buffet of food, but all he could afford was his ticket. The captain looked at him in amazement and said, "Didn't you know that the price of your ticket included your meals in the dining room?"

Maybe you have been living on cheese and crackers your whole life and you're looking forward to Heaven, not realizing that your ticket to Heaven includes everything you need on your way there. When Jesus bought your salvation passage to Heaven, He included everything you would need in your spirit, soul, body, family, and finances in this earth.

RECEIVING GOD'S INHERITANCE

In Luke 15, the elder brother never saw himself in a position that his father would love him enough to share with him. But think about it! The father loved his son so much, he even shared his inheritance with a son who was disobedient. That is fulfillment of Scripture. God is so good He lets the rain fall on the just and on the unjust. He has even blessed wicked people on this earth with food to eat, with air to breathe, and with so many other good things. Why? He's a good God all the time.

It is my prayer that you would have a revelation of your Father's love and your position as His child. When you know that you are a son or a daughter of God, you will walk in a place of blessing and in a place of authority. You may have relegated yourself to being like a worm, a dirty dog, or nothing more than a servant. God has called us His friends, and He has made every born-again believer His son or His daughter. So we have a different position. When we understand that, everything will change: how we think about ourselves; how we think about others; how we pray; how we work, play, worship, and live; and how we relate to others. The Spirit of God is bringing this revelation to people who will hear His voice.

First John 3:1-,2 says:

Behold what manner of love the Father has bestowed on us, that we should be called children of God! Therefore the world does not know us, because it did not know Him.

Beloved, now we are children of God; and it has not yet been revealed what we shall be, but we know that when He is revealed, we shall be like Him, for we shall see Him as He is.

When you were born again, you were born in the nature of the Father, just as the nature of the parents goes into their children in the natural realm. When you received the seed of the Word of God in your heart, your spirit gave birth to God's life in you. You have been made like Him in your spirit, and every day He is working on getting what is on the inside of you to the outside of you.

You are a child of the Most High God, a King's kid! The love that is in the Father is now in you. The joy that is in the Father is now in you. The righteousness that is in Jesus Christ is in you. You have become partakers of His divine nature.

First John 4:4 says, "You are of God, little children, and have overcome them, because He who is in you is greater than he who is in the world." You have been born of God. John 1:12 says, "But as many as received Him, to them He gave the right to become children of God, to those who believe in His name."

What does this mean? In the Old Testament, the person who could get the closest to God was the high priest. Once a year he would take the blood of an animal and go into a closed-off area called the "holy of holies," the place of God's presence. He would tiptoe into the holy of holies with bells on the hem of his garment and a rope around his leg because if he messed up, he would die in God's presence. Everyone else was outside of God's presence. No one even thought about being a child of God. It was impossible because we had a sin nature in us and God is holy. To be a child of God because of Jesus' death, burial, and resurrection is the greatest thing on the earth to celebrate!

Think about the children of Sam Walton. Because of his great entrepreneurial skills for developing a business, he built the huge empire of Sam's Clubs and Wal-Mart stores. Children of Sam Walton inherited a huge chunk of stock, and that stock has increased in value over the years. All of those relatives are millionaires because of their father's ability.

Don't be envious or jealous of people on this earth. Your heavenly Father owns it all! Not only are you blessed here on this earth, but you have a promise of eternal life with God. You are an heir of God and a joint heir with Jesus Christ (see Rom. 8:17).

Some people wonder what will happen to them when they die. When faced with death, George Harrison, one of the Beatles, said, "What happens when you die? Everything else is secondary." I do not know if he made a commitment to Jesus or not, but one thing I am confident of is, if you are a child of God (you have accepted Jesus Christ as your Lord and Savior), you are going to live forever in the presence of the Lord in Heaven. Death cannot keep you, and the grave cannot hold you.

You may have come from a bad family life, a broken home, rejection, abandonment, or perhaps you were an orphan. Maybe you came from a good family life. You had a good father. Maybe you were raised by a single parent, but you had it good. It doesn't matter where you came from. Today you have a heavenly Father who loves you, receives you, and accepts you.

In Colossians 1:12-13, Paul says that God has qualified you to be a partaker of His inheritance:

Giving thanks to the Father who has qualified us to be partakers of the inheritance of the saints in the light. [God qualified us for His inheritance when we accepted His Son, Jesus Christ, as our Lord and Savior.]

He has delivered us from the power of darkness and conveyed us into the kingdom of the Son of His love.

It is in Jesus that we have redemption. That means He purchased us with His blood and He has forgiven our sins.

Those who race in the Indianapolis 500 have to be qualified by their race car performance. They are qualified by the driver's ability and record. It's the same way with the PGA Championship. You are ranked according to the tournaments you have won. This is true with many sports.

In the spiritual arena, there is no way we can qualify ourselves to be a part of God's family. But God loved us so much that He sent His Son to pay for our sins to qualify us so we could get into His family once we accept Jesus as our Lord and Savior. We couldn't even get on the track, much less get in the race, by our own efforts. Jesus got on the track and ran the race for us all the way to the cross so we could be a part of the family of God.

In Romans 8:16-17, Paul said:

The Spirit Himself bears witness with our spirit that we are children of God, and if children, then heirs—heirs of God and joint heirs with Christ, if indeed we suffer with Him, that we may also be glorified together.

When I married Sharon, I was accepted into the Swift family. Her father had been my pastor at Asbury United Methodist Church in Magnolia, Arkansas, where we grew up, and her mother had been my youth pastor. Her brother David had been a good friend, and Sharon and I were in the same youth group. Because of grace, I was accepted into their family.

It was the grace of God that got you into His family. You can come boldly into God's presence. Whatever you need, He has it for you.

A good earthly father will do everything in his power to meet the needs of his children—food, clothing, medical care, housing, etc. A good earthly father will protect his children from bullies who threaten to hurt them.

Our heavenly Father is greater than anything you can imagine of the best earthly fathers. He will fight for you. He will provide for you. He will love you. He will give you what you need. It is time for you to be confident that you can enter God's presence with boldness.

> *It doesn't matter where you came from.*
>
> *Today you have a heavenly Father who loves you, receives you, and accepts you.*

Years ago I was meeting with several people to look over the drawings on a building we were getting ready to construct. We had the drawings spread out on the floor. Our oldest son John was very young. He left his school classroom in the same building and came to see me about a need he had. He walked in, stomped all over those plans, and crawled up in my lap. How could he do that? He's my son! You say, "Did I get mad at him?" No, I loved on him and took care of the situation that he was facing. Since then I have taught him to recognize people who are in a room and not stomp on everything, but the point is, the door is still open to him.

Many people's mentality is that God's door is closed to them. It's time to get a revelation! Your heavenly Father has opened His door to you! He loves you, He cares about you, and He has a great plan for your life.

ACCEPTED IN THE BELOVED

In Ephesians 1:3-6, Paul says:

Blessed be the God and Father of our Lord Jesus Christ, who has blessed us with every spiritual blessing in the heavenly places in Christ,

just as He chose us in Him before the foundation of the world, that we should be holy and without blame before Him in love,

having predestined us to adoption as sons by Jesus Christ to Himself, according to the good pleasure of His will,

to the praise of the glory of His grace, by which He made us accepted in the Beloved.

You may have felt like an outcast or a nobody, but now you have been adopted as a child of God right into His family.

You may be alone in a dorm room, in an apartment, or on a job, but you are not alone and without God. There may not be other people around you to support you, but the God of the universe has committed Himself to you as a heavenly Father. God created the world and the earth for you to live in with you in mind. Then He gave His most priceless possession for you, His Son, Jesus Christ.

KNOWING GOD AS FATHER

Romans 8:31-32 says:

If God is for us, who can be against us? He who did not spare His own Son, but delivered Him up for us all, how shall He not with Him also freely give us all things?

I remember when I was in a state college in Arkansas and someone talked to me about Oral Roberts University. The Holy Spirit spoke inside of me that I was to attend O.R.U., but there was no way in the natural. I had no money, and my family had little money.

I had received Christ as my Lord and Savior, but I was eating cheese and crackers all the way!

I knew a young man who was attending O.R.U. and wondered how he could afford it because his family was as poor as my family was at that time. I asked, "Ken, how are you attending O.R.U.?" He looked at me and said, "God is my Father, and He owns the cattle on a thousand hills and the oil and gas under those hills. If He calls me to do something, He will meet *all* of my needs according to His riches in glory by Christ Jesus."

My world exploded! I had been living in a tiny little matchbox, and now suddenly I was connecting with the God who hung the moon and the stars! He's not some faraway God. He's my Daddy. He knows me. I can step on the papers and come right up into His lap, just as my son John did with me.

Why did Jesus come? God wanted you in His lap. He wanted you in His family. How do we know this? The Word of God tells us so. Jesus also sent the Holy Spirit to us, He poured God's love into us, and now we can love other people with His love.

LOVE CORRECTS

God disciplines, chastens, corrects, rebukes, and reproves us, just as a natural, loving father does with his children. Do you ever remember your dad saying, "I'm doing this because I love you"? Your thought was probably, *Don't love me so much!*

Hebrews 12:5-6 says, "My son, do not despise the chastening of the Lord, nor be discouraged when you are rebuked by Him; for whom the Lord loves He chastens, and scourges every son whom He receives."

You know that God loves you and that you are His child because He rebukes, reproves, corrects, chastens, and disciplines you. The result of your obedience to His chastening is that you repent, change, and turn from going your own way to going God's way. You alter your course. You adjust and repair. You make amends. You make a turnaround. That's how you know you are a son or a daughter of God.

Have you had the Lord correct you? Or, have you had the Holy Spirit speak to you, saying: "That's wrong. Change it. Adjust your path. Get rid of that sin. Get that attitude out of your life"?

If you are not hearing that and you are not making adjustments and repenting regularly, you might have religion instead of a relationship, because a relationship includes both sides of this coin. On one side, the blessing side, is authority; but on the other side is discipline, correction, and training. Why? God is raising you to be a son or a daughter who is going to work in the family business!

Jesus said, "I must be about My Father's business" (Luke 2:49). The Father has a business. It's the family business, so everyone in the family is in this business.

Hebrews 12:7-11 continues on the topic of the discipline and correction of love:

If you endure chastening, God deals with you as with sons; for what son is there whom a father does not chasten?

But if you are without chastening, of which all have become partakers, then you are illegitimate and not sons. [The writer of Hebrews makes it really clear that if you are not being disciplined that results in repentance and change, you are not a child of God.]

Furthermore, we have had human fathers who corrected us, and we paid them respect. Shall we not much more readily be in subjection to the Father of spirits and live?

For they [our earthly fathers] *indeed for a few days chastened us as seemed best to them, but He for our profit, that we may be partakers of His holiness.* [Our earthly fathers disciplined us and our heavenly Father does so we can be partakers of His holiness.]

Now no chastening seems to be joyful for the present, but painful; nevertheless, afterward it yields the peaceable fruit of righteousness to those who have been trained by it.

Notice, the result of accepting and responding to God's chastening is that you will be a partaker of His holiness and you will enjoy the peaceable fruit of righteousness. When correction results in obedience to God's Word, His blessings will chase you down!

CHAPTER 11

YOUR OBEDIENCE RESULTS IN BLESSINGS, YOUR DISOBEDIENCE IN CURSES

Further knowledge of God being your answer, not your problem, is found in Galatians, chapter 3. Paul tells us that Jesus hung on the tree at Calvary to provide the way for every person who would believe in Him to become a son or a daughter of God. As a child of God, we are Abraham's seed or an heir, and the blessing of Abraham is ours:

Christ has redeemed us from the curse of the law, having become a curse for us (for it is written, "Cursed is everyone who hangs on a tree"),

that the blessing of Abraham might come upon the Gentiles in Christ Jesus, that we might receive the promise of the Spirit through faith (Galatians 3:13-14).

It is important to understand that in God's way of thinking there are three classes of people: Jews, Gentiles, and the Church (see 1 Cor. 10:32). Jews are those who had a covenant with God through Abraham. Gentiles are those without a covenant. The Church is the group that has accepted Jesus Christ as the Son of God crucified, buried, and resurrected. When God speaks of Jews,

Gentiles, and the Church, He is talking about the whole world. The blessing that God promised to Abraham and to his descendants can now come upon people who aren't natural seeds of Abraham, but they have been brought into that lineage through faith in Jesus Christ.

For you are all sons of God through faith in Christ Jesus.

For as many of you as were baptized into Christ have put on Christ.

There is neither Jew nor Greek, there is neither slave nor free, there is neither male nor female; for you are all one in Christ Jesus (Galatians 3:26-28).

The point Paul is making is that whether you were a natural descendant of Abraham or not, whether you are a man or a woman, whether you are slave or free, every person has an opportunity to be a child of God. We become one with Christ and one in the family of God through faith in Jesus Christ. "And if you are Christ's, then you are Abraham's seed, and heirs according to the promise" (Gal. 3:29).

An heir is a beneficiary, someone who receives a blessing from another person, someone who receives an inheritance such as a child would receive from a parent. As born-again believers, we are beneficiaries of the goodness of God that He promised to Abraham. Everything He promised to Abraham is available to us.

There is a principle at work all the way through the Bible, and that is: If you obey, there is a blessing; but if you disobey, there is a curse. When Adam and Eve ate of the tree that God had forbidden them to eat from, there were consequences. God gave a law through Moses. If the people obeyed, there were blessings. If they disobeyed, there were curses. So, very simply, if you obey God's Word, there is a blessing; but if you disobey, there is a curse.

Because we are descendants of Adam, not one of us in our natural ability can totally obey God unless Jesus helps us. So every human being was put in the same category of sin. Paul said it in Romans 3:23: "For all have sinned and fall short of the glory of God."

All of us, apart from the blessing of God, were affected by the curse. We needed to be set free. We needed someone to take our place, and that's what Jesus did. He came to redeem us from the curse. That's the goodness of God! "Redeem" means bought back, purchased, or ransomed. In a kidnapping situation, many times a ransom is demanded and paid to free someone from captivity. We were held captive to satan and to sin, and the effect of that was the curse. We needed someone to liberate us.

First Peter 1:18-19 says that we were not redeemed with silver and gold, but with the precious blood of Jesus Christ. There was no earthly price that could be paid to free us. It had to be holy, pure, spotless blood. God had set the decree, "If you sin, you will die." That was the Supreme Court decision made by the Judge of the Universe!

The life of any human being is in the blood. So when Jesus gave His blood, He gave His life and accepted death in our place to free us from satanic captivity. According to First Corinthians 6:20, we were bought with a price. That puts us in a different category. No longer do we belong to ourselves, but *we belong to Almighty God.*

If you obey God's Word, there is a blessing; but if you disobey, there is a curse.

As a result of Jesus' redeeming us, or paying the price to purchase us, we are redeemed from the curse of the law. The curse of breaking God's law began in the Garden with Adam and Eve, but it didn't stop there. All through history we see the result of people breaking God's law, and as a result the curse coming upon them. This became very clear when Moses revealed God's specific laws in Deuteronomy 28. He said, "If you do these things, these blessings will come upon you. If you don't do them, then these curses will come upon you." You can read the blessings in verses 1-14 and the curses in verses 15-68.

SEVEN CATEGORIES OF CURSES

A curse comes as a result of disobedience to God's laws. The curses, which come from the enemy, are in total opposition to God's blessings.

Instead of going through the 54 verses of curses, I will give you seven categories that these curses fall under.

1. *The curse for breaking God's law is bondage to sin.* Sin produces more sin and brings captivity where people become slaves to satan.

2. *The curse for breaking God's law is sickness and disease.* When Moses began to write these curses, he talked about blindness, deafness, cancer, consumption, pestilence, and all types of diseases. Then he said, "And any other diseases I didn't name."

3. *The curse for breaking God's law is broken marriages and families.* Moses said that disobedience to God's law would cause people's children to go into captivity. In Moses' day the captivity was to the Babylonians or to the Egyptians. Today, captivity is to drugs, alcohol, immorality, crime, and rebellion. Homes are being destroyed and families are being ripped apart.

4. *The curse for breaking God's law included poverty and lack.* If you were under the curse, God said you would borrow and you would not be in a position to lend. Lands and homes would be taken away because of a lack of finances. The heavens would be like brass, and the ground like powder. Nothing would produce, so there would be constant lack.

5. *Another curse for disobeying God's law is mental torment.* Mental torment includes confusion, oppression, and insanity.

6. *Another curse for disobeying God's law is failure rather than success.* They would go to battle one way and their enemies would cause them to flee seven ways. God said, "Whatever you put your hand to do, it will fail. It will not prosper."

7. *Another curse for disobeying God is spiritual death or separation from God forever.*

JESUS TOOK OUR CURSE

Our curse was laid upon Jesus at the cross. He took the penalty for our sins.

Isaiah 53:5, First Peter 2:24, and Matthew 8:16-17 say that Jesus bore our sicknesses and He carried our diseases. At the cross Jesus was separated from His own family. His mother wept at the foot of the cross. In Second Corinthians 8:9, Paul says that Jesus "became poor, that you through His poverty might become rich." Isaiah 53:5 says, "The chastisement for our peace was upon Him."

The day Jesus wore the crown of thorns was the day He wore our curse mentally. He took the torment in His mind. He also took the humiliation of rejection and being crucified. He took the humiliation of what appeared to be failure and defeat, although it was turned to absolute victory!

Jesus took our *total curse* at the cross—spirit, soul, body, family, and finances. He suffered in our place. Why? He took our sin so that we could be made righteous. He took our sickness so we could have health in our body. He took the brokenness of home and family so we could enjoy harmony and unity. He took our poverty and lack so we could have His abundance, prosperity, and blessing. Jesus took oppression and torment in His mind so we could have peace, tranquility, and joy.

Jesus took failure at the cross and on the third day He was raised from the dead and won the victory over death, hell, and the grave so we could have His victory. Jesus took our death so we could have eternal life with Him. We have been redeemed from the curse.

Every believer can have the presence of God in their life.

In Genesis 12:2-3, God said to Abram:

> *I will make you a great nation; I will bless you and make your name great; and you shall be a blessing.*
>
> *I will bless those who bless you, and I will curse him who curses you; and in you all the families of the earth shall be blessed.*

Genesis 24:1 says, "Now Abraham was old, well advanced in age; and the Lord had blessed Abraham in all things." Abraham was blessed in every area of his life. Every time he went into battle he was victorious. He was blessed with a relationship with God, and God credited his faith as righteousness.

The blessing of Abraham comes on you through your faith in Jesus Christ. When you put faith in the blood of the Lamb, you enter into a New Covenant relationship, but you also receive the promises God made to the man Abraham with whom He first made covenant.

In the Old Covenant, sin was covered; but in the New Covenant, our sins are removed. In the Old Covenant, people could approach God only through a priest. But today every believer can have the presence of God in their life. We don't just go into His presence. His presence comes into us at our salvation experience. Again it is obvious: God is our answer, not our problem!

THE BLESSINGS FOR OBEDIENCE

The blessings God promised to Abraham and his descendants are given in Deuteronomy 28:1-14. Let's look at these blessings.

Now it shall come to pass, if you diligently obey the voice of the Lord your God, to observe carefully all His commandments which I command you today, that the Lord your God will set you high above all nations of the earth. [God planned for His people to be on top, not on the bottom.]

And all these blessings shall come upon you and overtake you, because you obey the voice of the Lord your God. (Deuteronomy 28: 1-2).

The only way you can obey God's Word is through faith in Jesus Christ and through the Holy Spirit working on the inside of you. To be "blessed" means to prosper, to increase, to be satisfied and fulfilled.

Blessed shall you be in the city, and blessed shall you be in the country. [You will be blessed wherever you live.]

Blessed shall be the fruit of your body [your children], *the produce of your ground* [your crops] *and the increase of your herds, the increase of your cattle and the offspring of your flocks* [your livelihood].

Blessed shall be your basket and your kneading bowl. [In other words, you are going to have plenty to eat.]

Blessed shall you be when you come in, and blessed shall you be when you go out. [If you don't know whether you are coming or going, you are blessed either way.]

The Lord will cause your enemies who rise against you to be defeated before your face; they shall come out against you one way and flee before you seven ways. [You will have victory over the enemy.]

The Lord will command the blessing on you in your storehouses [Notice, plural "storehouses"! Today your storehouses are your savings and checking accounts.] *and in all to which you set your hand, and He will bless you in the land which the Lord your God is giving you.*

The Lord will establish you as a holy people to Himself [that means He is working His holiness in you], *just as He has sworn to you, if you keep the commandments of the Lord your God and walk in His ways.*

Then all peoples of the earth shall see that you are called by the name of the Lord, and they shall be afraid [in awe] *of you* (Deuteronomy 28:3-10).

People will be in awe of the blessings upon your life. Why am I telling you this? You won't rise any higher than your vision. If your vision is of always being poor, in debt, having sickness in the family, having some area of sin controlling you, being in oppression, confusion, or darkness, then you will live in that realm. Many people today, even though they are Christians, think that is their lot in life because no one ever told them they have been freed in Christ Jesus.

You can have money in the bank in your name, but if you don't know about it or you don't make a withdrawal on it, that money will never do you any good. God has put more than money in the bank for you. He has put the blessing of Abraham in an account for you. *But you must make a withdrawal on it to lay hold of these blessings.*

And the Lord will grant you plenty of goods [the things that you need], *in the fruit of your body* [that's your children], *in the increase of your livestock* [your animals], *and in the produce of your ground* [your crops], *in the land of which the Lord swore to your fathers to give you.*

The Lord will open to you His good treasure, the heavens, to give the rain to your land in its season, and to bless all the work of your hand. You shall lend to many nations, but you shall not borrow. [Part of the curse is being in bondage to debt. The blessing is to be free from debt.]

And the Lord will make you the head and not the tail; you shall be above only, and not be beneath, if you heed the commandments of the Lord your God, which I command you today, and are careful to observe them.

So you shall not turn aside from any of the words which I command you this day, to the right or to the left, to go after other gods to serve them. (Deuteronomy 28:11-14).

Jesus took our curse so that once we are born again, we can walk in obedience and receive the blessing of Abraham. It's important that you receive these blessings and understand that this is how you are supposed to live. Even if your family has never lived in the blessing realm, you can go there. To live in abundance is God's plan for you.

We will live on the level of our core belief system. You can pray for people to be healed, but if sickness is a way of life in their mind, although they may be temporarily healed, they will go back and walk in sickness. Someone can pray for God to meet your financial needs, but if in your mind-set you see yourself in poverty as a way of life, you will go back and do without.

If we pray for you to have victory in a situation you are facing and you receive that victory, if your mind-set is defeat as a way of life, you will go back and live in defeat.

We have to change our whole belief and thinking systems in our heart and in our mind to say, "I am redeemed." This is a legal transaction. The Supreme Court of the Universe has settled this deal. Your debt has been paid. Your liberty has been bought. The blood of Jesus Christ is on the books. You are free. You can rise up into complete victory in every area of your life. It's a choice. You see, God is not your problem. He is your Answer!

ISRAELITES' DELIVERANCE OUT OF EGYPT

When the children of Israel called out to God and reminded Him of the promises He made to Abraham, the Bible says that He remembered and He called forth a deliverer whose name was Moses. Ten supernatural miracles happened. The final miracle was when God told the Israelites to kill a lamb and sprinkle its blood on the doorposts, and the angel of death would pass over the house where he saw the blood applied.

The Egyptians did not trust in the blood of a lamb, and that night the firstborn son in every Egyptian home died. When Pharaoh's son was found dead, Pharaoh arose and said to Moses, "Get your people and get out of here!" In one night they were delivered.

When you trust in the blood of the Lamb, death may be all around you, but you will be delivered out of that bondage. I believe the deliverance of the Israelites out of Egypt is the most powerful story in the Old Testament.

Pharaoh represented satan, and the land represented the demonic host oppressing God's people. Then a deliverer came representing Jesus Christ. Moses said that a prophet would be raised up to deliver them. Jesus worked signs, wonders, and miracles. He gave His blood. Moses just told the people, "Get a lamb," but Jesus is the Lamb.

That night when the Israelites came out of Egypt, they passed through the Red Sea because God divided it, then buried their enemies under those same waters. Moses said, "Do not be afraid. Stand still, and see the salvation of the Lord, which He will accomplish for you today. For the Egyptians whom you see today, you shall see again no more forever. The Lord will fight for you, and you shall hold your peace" (Exod. 14:13-14).

This is under the blessing of Abraham. Remember, today we not only have the blessing of Abraham, but we have the New Covenant too. Christ redeemed us from the curse so the blessing of Abraham could come on us. If you have received Jesus Christ as your Lord and Savior, you are now a son or a daughter of God. You are in the New Covenant.

Psalm 105 tells about the Israelites' deliverance out of Egypt. Let's look at verses 37-45:

He also brought them out with silver and gold, and there was none feeble among His tribes. [Imagine a mass healing service of three million people healed in one night!]

Egypt was glad when they departed, for the fear of them had fallen upon them.

He spread a cloud for a covering [divine protection], *and fire to give light in the night* [His divine presence].

The people asked, and He brought quail, and satisfied them with the bread of heaven [divine provision].

He opened the rock, and water gushed out; it ran in the dry places like a river. [Jehovah Jireh had already seen ahead and made provision for them.]

For He remembered His holy promise [word or covenant commitment], *and Abraham His servant.*

God made a promise to Abraham. These are the descendants of Abraham, and God fulfilled His promise. God will remember His promise to Abraham on your behalf.

Psalm 105:43-45 say:

He brought out His people with joy, His chosen ones with gladness.

He gave them the lands of the Gentiles, and they inherited the labor of the nations;

that they might observe His statutes and keep His laws.

Why has God redeemed us? He wants a people for Himself, a people who will love Him, honor Him, obey Him, and serve Him. We have been redeemed for a holy purpose.

LET THE REDEEMED OF THE LORD SAY SO!

To live in the blessing of Abraham in every area of your life, you must know that you have been redeemed from the curse of the law, believe it, and then enforce it. The devil will try to tell you that you are still under the curse. This is why you must enforce his defeat with the truth of God's Word believed in your heart and spoken from your mouth.

If the postman comes to your house and says, "I've got a package of sickness and disease for you," you can tell him, "You have the wrong address. I am not signing for that package, because a new creation lives in this house!"

When he comes with poverty and lack, you have to rise up and decree that you are redeemed from it. Psalm 107:2 is your key verse: "Let the redeemed of the Lord say so...." The enemy will run over you if you don't enforce God's Word.

> *It is important for you to declare that you are redeemed.*

When Jesus was tempted by the devil, He rose up and declared the Word of God. He said, "It is written," and then quoted specific Scripture that applied to the temptation. (See Matthew 4:1-11.) You and I must declare, *It is written, we are redeemed.* If satan comes with a package of poverty or a package of torment for you, you can declare, *I'm not signing for that anymore. I am redeemed.*

Revelation 12:11 says, "And they overcame him [the accuser of the brethren] by the blood of the Lamb and by the word of their testimony, and they did not love their lives to the death."

"The blood of the Lamb" is talking about your redemption. Declare it. The blood of Jesus Christ stops satan. Remember, His blood freed you from satan's dominion. Jesus' blood freed you from the curse. You can know it, but until you declare it, it is not enforced. Every day you need to declare, *I am redeemed.*

When people ask you, "Who are you?" no longer identify yourself as just a businessman, a housewife, a businesswoman, or by where you work, live, or even by your name. Just tell them, *I am redeemed. That's who I am.* Why? Because that's your identity that will cause you one day to stand before the King of kings and sing a song that only the redeemed can sing.

We have to enforce satan's defeat and enforce our redemption. As you begin to declare it, wisdom will come to you in your business. Healing will come to your body. The works of the enemy that would try to rip your home apart will be stopped. God will bring harmony and peace. It is important for you to declare that you are redeemed.

Years ago, saints would pray over their wagons and say, "We plead the blood of Jesus around this wagon." You ought to do that around your wagon! It probably has a motor in it today. They would say, "We plead the blood of Jesus around this home." What were they doing? They were declaring their redemption rights: By the blood of Jesus, we have divine protection.

> *The enemy cannot attack*
> *our home and family.*
> *No falling meteors,*
> *no earthquakes or volcanoes,*
> *no lies of the devil will prosper against us.*

You need to plead the blood of Jesus over your mind. *No torment, confusion, or insanity is going to come in my mind. By the blood of Jesus, I have the mind of Christ.* At times, every person has to resist wrong thoughts, torment, and confusion. I am speaking to you to rise up in your inner man and resist the devil and lay claim to your redemption rights.

The whole Bible is the story of our redemption. We were born to be with God. Sin came and we went into captivity, but Jesus came and set us free. He redeemed us.

The devil will come to you and say, "You're a dirty rat. Look what you

By the blood of Jesus, we have divine protection.

By the blood of Jesus, I have the mind of Christ.

thought. Look what you said. You wicked thing! Look what you did. You don't deserve to be healed." He will tell you, "You don't deserve to be prosperous. You don't deserve to succeed." He will point out your sin. He is the accuser of the brethren. He is the prosecuting attorney, and he is presenting his case.

But, at the right hand of the Judge, the Counsel for our defense arises and takes the stand. He says, "I have evidence that I want to present. My blood is on the altar."

Begin to declare,

My Redeemer lives!
I am redeemed in my mind.
I am redeemed in my body.
I am redeemed in my heart.
I am redeemed
by the blood of the Lamb in my finances.
I am redeemed from torment.
My family
is redeemed from being ripped apart.
I am redeemed from iniquity.
Sin will not rule over my life
in the name of Jesus Christ of Nazareth.

Rise up in your inner man. You were not born for the mud hole. You were not born to live in sin, sickness, poverty, or bondage. You were born to walk as a king under the kingship of the Lord Jesus. You are the redeemed because of the blood of the Lamb.

CHAPTER 12

RISE UP AND KEEP ON GOING!

Every person at some point in their life has taken a "hit" that struck in such a way that they felt like they were down for the count! A friendship gone wrong. Sickness or disease in you or in a family member. A financial reversal. A job layoff or unexpected change.

Discouragement, among other things, is designed to take you down and out. These obstacles are *not* designed by God. I am talking about the works of the enemy, the spirit of this age, the world's system that moves against God's people. It's important for you to know how to rise up with Jesus no matter what comes your way.

Sometimes we are hit with persecution for our faith. At other times we are hit with an attack or with a temptation. Then there are times that we face trials, difficulties, and problems that arise because of what we are doing in our family, in our business, or even in what we are doing for God.

When the apostle Paul faced situations like this, he said:

But this precious treasure—this light and power that now shine within us—is held in a perishable container, that is, in our weak bodies. Everyone can see that the glorious power within must be from God and is not our own.

We are pressed on every side by troubles, but not crushed and broken. We are perplexed because we don't know why things happen as they do, but we don't give up and quit. We are hunted down, but God never abandons us. We get knocked down, but we get up again and keep going. These bodies of ours are constantly facing death just as Jesus did; so it is clear to all that it is only the living Christ within [who keeps us safe].

Yes, we live under constant danger to our lives because we serve the Lord, but this gives us constant opportunities to show forth the power of Jesus Christ within our dying bodies. (2 Corinthians 4:7-11 TLB).

What a powerful word! Though we get knocked down, we get up and keep on going. The good news is, *we have resurrection power in us!*

Any person who has walked with God has been through tests, trials, hits, and knocks! You may be hurting on the inside, even though it appears you are standing up on the outside. There may be a story that only you know about and because of it, there is deep pain in your life. This is the day for getting up and rising above the storm that has hit your life.

> *Whatever you are facing, this is your day to rise up!*

You may be a teenager struggling with comparison, competition, or fears of the future. Because of the scrutiny or the judgment of your friends and peers, you feel discouraged and put down. You may be a senior citizen and you are facing situations with family and with your own health that have tried to discourage you and rob you of joy. Whatever you are facing, *this is your day to rise up!*

Because we are earthen vessels in pots of clay, we don't have the strength in ourselves to rise up. We can't rise up in our own ability. Paul was beaten, shipwrecked, and jailed for the gospel. Possibly he faced more persecution than anyone we know other than Jesus Christ Himself. Yet Paul said, "I keep rising up."

Micah put it this way: "Do not rejoice over me, my enemy; when I fall, I will arise; when I sit in darkness, the Lord will be a light to me" (Mic. 7:8). When darkness tries to invade your life or your home, God says, "I will be your light!" Psalm 27:1 says, "The Lord is my light and my salvation…."

The Spirit of God is going to minister something in you that you will be able to impart to other people. On a daily basis, most of us encounter people who have been hit in one way or another. They are struggling. They may show it in their faces; others may try to hide it, but within their heart, there is pain from something that has hit their life. Micah said, "If something happens and I get knocked down, I will arise!"

If you think like Paul or Micah, you are unsinkable! Have you ever been out in a lake or in a swimming pool and you put an inflatable ball under the water? It pops right back up. You push it down and it pops back up. That's like you and me. The devil may try to put us under, but we keep popping right back up. This is similar to a boxer who has been knocked down for the count. The referee is counting, but there is resurrection life coming up on the inside of this person! Begin to confess, *I shall arise!*

THE EPHESIANS 1 PRAYER OF PAUL

In Ephesians 1, Paul prayed for his friends. This prayer is for anyone who will receive it:

Therefore I also, after I heard of your faith in the Lord Jesus and your love for all the saints,

do not cease to give thanks for you, making mention of you in my prayers:

That the God of our Lord Jesus Christ, the Father of glory, may give to you the spirit of wisdom and revelation in the knowledge of Him,

the eyes of your understanding being enlightened [that's your spirit, your inner man, your heart]; *that you may know what is the hope of His calling, what are the riches of the glory of His inheritance in the saints,*

and what is the exceeding greatness of His power toward us who believe, according to the working of His mighty power

which He worked in Christ when He raised Him from the dead and seated Him at His right hand in heavenly places,

far above all principality and power and might and domin- ion, and every name that is named, not only in this age but also in that which is to come.

And He put all things under His feet, and gave Him to be head over all things to the church,

which is His body, the fullness of Him who fills all in all (Ephesians 1:15-23).

Paul lists three things he really wants us to know:

1. *The hope of His calling* (Eph. 1:18). This is referring to what God has called or assigned us to do in this earth.

2. *What are the riches of the glory of His inheritance in the saints* (Eph. 1:18). An inheritance is something that is left to us by someone who has something to give. God has something to give to us. In Christ He has given us all the treasures of the Kingdom of God. In Jesus Christ we have life, love, peace, joy, victory, provision, health, wholeness, strength, and protection.

    If you hear that a very rich relative has left you a huge portion of their inheritance, would you do anything to try to discover what was in that person's will? It is your inheritance. It has your name on it. It is assigned specifically to you. The executor of that will comes to you and says, "I am here to help you." Would you give some attention and time to discovering your inheritance? That's what Paul is asking.

God has left us everything in His Son, Jesus Christ. Paul was saying, "I am praying that you will have a spirit of wisdom, revelation, knowledge, and understanding to know what is in your inheritance."

This is one of the reasons we come together to fellowship in church services. The Greek word for fellowship is *ekklesia*. This is one of the reasons we read the Bible every day. Every time you read it, you are getting new light on your inheritance.

3. *What is the exceeding greatness of His power toward us who believe* (Eph. 1:19)? If you do not know the power that God has made available to you, that power won't do you any good.

   This also refers to the power that is available inside of us—what He has put in us."

   How much power is on the inside of you? What kind of power? It is the same power that God used to raise Jesus from the dead. There is no power greater than the resurrection power that raised Jesus from the dead. That is the Spirit of the living God. That power is on the inside of us.

   Many times people are praying, "Oh, Lord, send the power," and He says, "I already sent My Son. I already gave you the resurrection power—My Holy Spirit—to live on the inside of you."

No wonder Paul did not pray for them to have more power. He prayed that they would get a revelation of the power that was already inside of them.

Ephesians 1:20-21 says that when Jesus was raised from the dead, He was seated at the right hand of the Father in heavenly places, "far above all principality and power and might and dominion…" (Eph. 1:21). This means that Jesus was raised far above the devil and every demon spirit of this age.

When Jesus was raised from the dead, not only did He destroy the power of the grave, He broke open the tomb and rose above death and all the power of the enemy. This means that the same power that defeated satan is now on the inside of you! You have satan-defeating power in your life! Demons are afraid of you and me. They are afraid of people who know they have power.

When you realize the power that is inside of you, you won't stay under the cloud of your circumstances anymore. You will rise up in Jesus' name.

MINING FOR GOLD IN GOD'S WORD

Your attitude will determine your altitude. The way you think will determine how you live. "For as he thinks in his heart, so is he…" (Prov. 23:7). This is why when we are born again, we must renew our mind with God's Word. According to Joshua 1:8, we are supposed to meditate on what God has said in His Word. The way we meditate on what God has said is to keep talking the Word.

Begin to confess God's Word:
I am rising up with Jesus.
I am rising above every principality, power, and might.

The same power that defeated satan is now on the inside of you!

> *I am rising above discouragement,*
> *turmoil, pain, and difficulties.*
> *God's resurrection power*
> *is raising me above fear.*
> *The resurrection power of God in me*
> *is raising me above the circumstances I am facing today.*

God's promises won't work for us simply by trying to pull ourselves up by our own bootstraps. We are basing this on a discovery we made when we got into the gold mining work. We began mining for gold in the Scriptures, and we found a vein of revelation! In that gold—the tested and tried Word of the living God—we discovered that we are one with Jesus Christ, and that when He was raised from the dead, we were raised. When He arose, we arose. When He triumphed over the devil, we triumphed over the devil. Hallelujah!

YOUR POSITION *IN CHRIST*

Ephesians 2 gives us a picture of the position of the born-again believer:

> *And you He made alive, who were dead in trespasses and sins, in which you once walked according to the course of this world, according to the prince of the power of the air, the spirit who now works in the sons of disobedience,*

> *among whom also we all once conducted ourselves in the lusts of our flesh, fulfilling the desires of the flesh and of the mind, and were by nature children of wrath, just as the others.*

> *But God, who is rich in mercy, because of His great love with which He loved us,*

> *even when we were dead in trespasses, made us alive together with Christ (by grace you have been saved),*

> *and raised us up together, and made us sit together in the heavenly places in Christ Jesus (Ephesians 2:1-6).*

This is your resurrection. You have been made to rise up. It's time for you to begin to say,

I rise up in the power of God.
I rise up in the love of God that's on the inside of me.
I rise up in the peace of God.
God has raised me up in Christ
so I rise up in that resurrection power.
I rise up in the strength and in the anointing of God.
I rise up in the healing power of the Lord.
I rise up in the ministry of angels.

It's time to rise up in every area of your life. You are like a postage stamp. You may have taken a lickin' but you are going to keep on sticking! You may feel so low you could do a pushup under a dime, but there is power on the inside of you. It may look like you are down for the count, but the same power that raised Christ from the dead is on the inside of you.

It's simply time to rise up and keep on going! But you say, "I have failed miserably, and I'm still a failure." The teaching in the next chapter should be an encouragement to you when you realize that God looked beyond the failures of the woman at the well and used her in a mighty way. He will do the same for you!

CHAPTER 13

WHAT IF YOU HAVE FAILED MISERABLY AND YOU ARE STILL IN FAILURE?

At a well in Samaria, Jesus met a woman who had been married five times and she was living in adultery. Instead of condemning her, Jesus addressed the real need in her, which was eternal life.

He began by asking her for a drink of water. She responded, "'How is it that You, being a Jew, ask a drink from me, a Samaritan woman?' For Jews have no dealings with Samaritans" (John 4:9). Jesus is not prejudiced against people because of their gender, nationality, or lifestyle. He sees value in every human being.

Jesus spoke, "If you knew the gift of God, and who it is who says to you, 'Give Me a drink,' you would have asked Him, and He would have given you living water" (John 4:10). Notice that Jesus did not attack her verbally. He did not reject her. He knew that her greatest need was a heart change. When she inquired about the living water, Jesus replied, "The water that I shall give him will become in him a fountain of water springing up into everlasting life" (John 4:14).

Jesus sees past your failures to what you can become. He is answer-focused rather than problem-focused. He spoke to the woman of her five husbands and the fact that she was living in immorality at that moment. Jesus did not condone her sin, but instead He offered her a better life. He gave her the opportunity of choosing to believe in Him as the Savior, the promised Messiah (see John 4:25-26).

This woman not only chose to believe in Jesus, she publicly declared to the people in her city that Jesus was the Christ (see John 4:29). She invited everyone to come and see Him.

Jesus is not prejudiced against people because of their gender, nationality, or lifestyle. He sees value in every human being.

Imagine this scene. Everyone in her village must have known of this woman's failures in marriage and her immoral lifestyle. Yet Jesus allowed her to be used as an evangelist proclaiming His salvation on the very day of her own conversion. How could Jesus use someone with such a sordid past?

This is the good news of Jesus: *He loves you just the way you are, yet He sees you for what you can become.* One divine encounter changed this woman forever. No doubt she had been to the well many times, but this time she met the Son of God.

Although Jesus knows all the facts about your past, He still loves you. He sees you sharing the living water with others who are dry on the inside. Not only does He offer you eternal life, He offers you a partnership in the Father's business.

Twelve disciples (men) went into the same village and there is no record of them inviting anyone to come and see Jesus at the well (see John 4:8,27-33). However, a five-time divorced woman brings the whole city to Jesus.

God has *big plans* for you. It may seem like you have wasted your life, but with Jesus you can make up for lost years in a short time. He will not reject you for your past failures. He welcomes you to come to Him and receive living water—Agua Viva!

JONAH, NINEVEH, AND GOD'S MERCY

God called Jonah to go and preach in Nineveh because of the wickedness of the people of that city. Jonah disobeyed God. The Bible says, "The Lord sent out a great wind on the sea, and there was a mighty tempest on the sea, so that the ship was about to be broken up" (Jon. 1:4).

Remember, God is not your problem. He was not against Jonah; in fact, He planned Jonah's rescue long before Jonah was thrown into the sea. "Now the Lord had prepared a great fish to swallow Jonah…" (Jon. 1:17).

If you sense you are in the belly of a whale, remember that Jonah repented and survived. This experience was not sent to destroy him, but to assist him in changing his mind to do God's will. You could call it a low-level, high intensity, sub-Mediterranean cruise, motivational seminar! Jonah experi-

Jesus sees past your failures to what you can become.

enced God's mercy forgiving his sin of disobedience in order that he might proclaim God's mercy for the Ninevites' disobedience.

Jonah did go to Nineveh preaching, "Yet forty days, and Nineveh shall be overthrown!" (Jon. 3:4). It is obvious that Jonah fully expected to see Nineveh completely destroyed. But God showed mercy on the city, when the people repented with fasting and prayer.

Even the words of coming destruction because of sin were sent wrapped in God's mercy. He wants to save you and me from self-destruction. The people of Nineveh had little knowledge of God. They certainly did not honor Him or worship Him. Yet God loved all of them.

It is not God's will that anyone should perish, "but that all should come to repentance" (2 Pet. 3:9). The prophetic warnings sent to nations, cities, and individuals are not sent because God wants to vent His anger, but rather to call people to repent and receive God's mercy. God truly is on your side, even when you have failed.

Why? What is the purpose of God being so good? His nature is good, and it is the goodness of God that leads men to repent (see Rom. 2:4).

It is obvious that Jonah did not understand God's goodness. He fully expected God to completely destroy Nineveh. However, the people of Nineveh had a heart change when they heard the preaching of Jonah. The king made a decree:

Let neither man nor beast, herd nor flock, taste anything; do not let them eat, or drink water.

But let man and beast be covered with sackcloth, and cry mightily to God; yes, let every one turn from his evil way and from the violence that is in his hands.

Who can tell if God will turn and relent, and turn away from His fierce anger, so that we may not perish? (Jonah 3:7-9)

God's view is of eternity. He sees the ultimate destiny of all those who reject Him. Hell is forever for those who reject Him. What may seem harsh or hard when God's warnings and wake-up calls come is really God's tender mercy sent to deliver people from eternal torment.

The result of Nineveh's repentance was God changing the verdict: "Then God saw their works, that they turned from their evil way; and God relented from the disaster that He had said He would bring upon them, and He did not do it" (Jon. 3:10).

Jonah was angry at God for this change. He acknowledged that God is "a gracious and merciful God, slow to anger and abundant in loving kindness, One who relents from doing harm" (Jon. 4:2). Yet, Jonah was so displeased that he wanted to die.

The last verse of the Book of Jonah reveals God's heart of love and compassion for people: "Should I not pity Nineveh, that great city, in which are more than one hundred and twenty thousand persons who cannot discern between their right hand and their left…" (Jon. 4:11).

As you turn from sin and turn to Him, you can walk into all He has for you.

You may wonder if God cares about you. Does He even know you exist? If He does, is He willing to help you? Would He use His power and ability to make a difference in your life?

Think about the situation of Nineveh. This group of people were godless, violent, perverted, immoral, sin-ruled, and without any knowledge of God's Word. The Lord not only knew who they were, but He knew their spiritual condition. God was so concerned with them that He sent a prophet to warn them of coming judgment. When Jonah disobeyed, God went to extraordinary lengths to get him to Nineveh. The moment they repented, God lifted the judgment.

God knows where you are. He wants the best for you. He is sending people your way to help you get on the right path. Even this book lets you know how much God loves you and wants the best for your life. As you turn from sin and turn to Him, you can walk into all He has for you.

CHAPTER 14

_____ THE GOODNESS _____
OF GOD

God is good (see Ps. 100:5). Throughout the Bible the truth of God's goodness is revealed. It is His nature. You can count on God being good. He never changes. He is always the same (see Mal. 3:6).

When you know someone's character or nature, then you can understand their words and actions. When others may misjudge or accuse that person falsely, you can give the accurate picture because you know the true nature of the one being accused.

God has been falsely accused on many occasions as the one bringing death, destruction, calamity, tragedy, or evil. We know that God does judge sin and He is a righteous, holy God. But before you jump too quickly to give God credit for disastrous events or terrible trials, please take time to consider these thoughts.

First, sin has a penalty in itself. Sin is like a seed. If it is planted, watered, and cultivated, it grows a harvest. Sin is a principle or law just as righteousness is a principle or law. Each one produces certain results if they are enacted or practiced. We understand that gravity is a law that works. If someone jumps out of a ten-story building and dies, it is not God's fault. He did not cause the death. It was not God's will.

There are lots of bad things that happen to people that are simply the result of people making wrong choices. Certain consequences go with certain actions. In stating this, I am not condemning people, but rather I am seeking to help you realize that God is not your problem.

Second, the earth is under the curse of sin and death that began with Adam and Eve's sin (see Gen. 3:1-19; Rom. 8:20-21).

The creation of Heaven and earth was originally good. Everything was beautiful and in harmony. Destructive weather or cataclysmic earth changes were not a part of God's purpose and plan. The sin of man caused the earth to be cursed (see Gen. 3:17-18).

What men have called "acts of God," referring to natural disasters such as hurricanes, tornados, earthquakes, and drought, are actually the result of man's original sin and its impact on the planet.

Earth's conditions were radically changed by the flood, which came because of man's sin in Noah's day. "The fountains of the great deep [were] broken up, and the windows of heaven were opened" (Gen. 7:11). The entire complexion of earth's surface changed as waters went over the highest mountains. Huge changes took place in the atmosphere that have altered the weather since that event.

> *Sin is like a seed. If it is planted, watered, and cultivated, it grows a harvest.*

The point is simple. God made everything to be good, but man's actions even to this day are still affecting the planet. God is a good God and He is not your problem. Creation reveals His goodness. The Bible states that each aspect of creation was good (see Gen. 1:4,10,12,18,21,25). When God looked at everything He had made "it was very good" (Gen. 1:31).

THE LORD IS GOOD

Oh, taste and see that the Lord is good... (Psalm 34:8).

Good and upright is the Lord... (Psalm 25:8).

No good thing will He withhold from those who walk uprightly (Psalm 84:11).

Yes, the Lord will give what is good; and our land will yield its increase (Psalm 85:12).

For the Lord is good; His mercy is everlasting (Psalm 100:5).

Bless the Lord, O my soul; and all that is within me, bless His holy name!

Bless the Lord, O my soul, and forget not all His benefits:

Who forgives all your iniquities, who heals all your diseases,

Who redeems your life from destruction, who crowns you with lovingkindness and tender mercies,

Who satisfies your mouth with good things, so that your youth is renewed like the eagle's (Psalm 103:1-5).

Notice all the good things God provides because He is good. If you focus on the goodness of God, you will live a life of rejoicing!

Oh, give thanks to the Lord, for He is good! For His mercy endures forever (Psalm 106:1).

Oh, that men would give thanks to the Lord for His goodness, and for His wonderful works to the children of men!

For He satisfies the longing soul, and fills the hungry soul with goodness (Psalm 107:8-9).

Take time to thank God for His goodness. Praise Him for His wonderful works. You have more to rejoice over than to complain about. As the old song says, "Count your blessings, name them one by one."

Praise the Lord, for the Lord is good… (Psalm 135:3).

The Lord is good to all, and His tender mercies are over all His works (Psalm 145:9).

When you know someone's character and nature, you will not receive an accusation against them that contradicts who they are. For example, I know my mother is kind and gentle with people. If someone said something different about her, I would question the character of the individual making the accusation rather than my mom. I know her. She is consistent.

How much more should we be persuaded of God's goodness and unchanging character. Why is it so important? You cannot put trust in someone if you are not sure of their view of you. How can you have faith in God if you think He is your problem or He is against you? We trust people when we are assured that they have no intent to do us harm.

This should open your thinking to know why millions of people have difficulty putting their trust in God. One of the big reasons is that they have been convinced that God is the author of many of the bad things happening to people. By revealing the truth of God's goodness, we can help prepare hearts to receive the Savior without doubt or suspicion about His character.

If you focus on the goodness of God, you will live a life of rejoicing!

MY PRAYER FOR YOU

*Father, we thank You that Your character is unchanging
and Your nature is love.
You do chasten, correct, or discipline us,
but You do it with Your Word,
Your Spirit, and through godly people.*

*We know there is persecution and opposition in the world,
but You are not the one sending it.
You send us help to be overcomers of it.
But even in a bad world
with difficult things that are happening,
You are still a loving God
reaching out to us and caring for us,
lifting, healing, delivering, and restoring.*

Thank You, Lord,
for removing traditional roadblocks to miracles
and the lies of the enemy of misinformation
that have come to warp our picture of You.
I pray that these imaginations
would be cast down in Jesus' name
and that we would see You
for who You are—high and lifted up,
King of the universe, Lover of our souls.
You have loved us with an everlasting love,
and You went the full measure of devotion
to give Your blood for us.

Jesus, we love You.
We thank You for Your mercy and grace.
Even when we have been unfaithful,
You have remained faithful
and You have never changed.
Even when we have failed,
You have held on to us.
You didn't send the fire and burn us on the spot.
You believed that we would repent and turn.
You said in Your Word that
judgment had not come
because You are not willing that any should perish,
but that all would come to repentance.

Lord, I pray that
we would receive Your chastening from Your Word

138

and Your Spirit
and that it would lead us to repentance.
I pray for a new day of obedience in our lives
and that we would leave no open doors
to the enemy.

Lord Jesus,
today we have new understanding
in light of the New Covenant
in which our judgment fell upon You.
Until that great and final judgment comes,
we have a time of mercy and grace.
I pray for forgiveness to flow like a mighty river.
Every generational curse that has been on homes and families,
I speak for it to be canceled today
so no curse can be passed on to future generations
in Jesus' name.

Thank You, Lord,
that every suspicion about Your character
is being removed from our thoughts.
Every attitude where we thought
You might be behind our problems and difficulties,
destroy it from our thinking and our believing.
Never again will we forget
what You did for us on the cross, Jesus!
Amen.

PERSONAL PRAYER OF COMMITMENT

Father,

because of the teaching in this book,

I now see You in a new light

as a God of love, mercy, grace, goodness,

and forgiveness—not as a "one strike and you're out" God!

I acknowledge Jesus Christ as Your Son,

and I believe He was crucified,

buried, and resurrected to free me

from the curse of sin, poverty,

sickness, and spiritual death.

I renounce every work of darkness

and I receive and confess You now, Jesus,

as my personal Lord and Savior.

Thank You, Jesus,
for paying the price in full
for my deliverance from all the bad things
satan has brought into the earth.
Your blood protects me from the effects of these bad things,
and in You I walk in absolute freedom
from all the works of the devil.

Thank You for empowering me with Your Spirit, Lord,
so I can be an overcomer and a soul-winner in this life,
making a difference for Your Kingdom
wherever You direct me to go.

Thank You, Lord Jesus,
for a new beginning in You today!

Signature: _____

Date: _____